From the pages of *Fine Homebuilding* magazine

SARAH SUSANKA
NOT SO BIG
SOLUTIONS
FOR Your Home

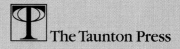The Taunton Press

For Christopher, whose brief time on this Earth awakened many to the joys of living in the present moment.

Text © 2002 by Sarah Susanka
Photos:
© Grey Crawford - pp. 12, 20, 24, 30, 34, 44, 48, 53, 60, 65, 88, 93, 99, 106, 111, 126, 131, 136, 141, 150
© Christian Korab - pp. 39, 115, 120
© Jeff Krueger - pp. 74, 78
© Karen Melvin - p. 70
© The Taunton Press, Inc., by Charles Miller, courtesy of *Fine Homebuilding* magazine - p. 16
© Sarah Susanka - pp. 8, 82
© Sarah Susanka while at Mulfinger, Susanka, Mahady & Partners - p. 145
Illustrations © 2002 by Sarah Susanka
Architect for the home featured on the cover - Jean Rehkamp Larson, Rehkamp Larson Architects
while at SALA Architects

The Taunton Press, Inc., 63 South Main Street, PO Box 5506, Newtown, CT 06470-5506

The Taunton Press
Inspiration for hands-on living™

e-mail: tp@taunton.com

Distributed by Publishers Group West

Jacket/Cover design: Anne Marie Manca
Interior design: Mary McKeon
Layout: Mary McKeon
Illustrator: Sarah Susanka and Christine Erikson

Library of Congress Cataloging-in-Publication Data
Susanka, Sarah.
    Not so big solutions for your home / Sarah Susanka.
        p. cm.
Contains articles originally written for "Fine homebuilding" magazine's
"Drawing board" column.
    ISBN 1-56158-613-7
    1. Architecture, Domestic--Designs and plans. 2. Interior
architecture--Designs and plans. 3. House construction. I. Fine
homebuilding. II. Title.
    NA7115 .S87 2002
    728'.37'0222--dc21

Printed in the United States of America
10 9 8 7 6 5 4 3 2 1

Acknowledgments

In 1987 a new editor at The Taunton Press's *Fine Homebuilding* magazine, Kevin Ireton, called me—a young architect in Minnesota—to ask if I would like to write an article for the magazine. I did so. It was well received, and it helped me realize that my calling was as much verbal as it was architectural. Thus began a collaborative journey with The Taunton Press that seems to grow and blossom with every passing year. Kevin went on to become Editor-in-Chief of *Fine Homebuilding*, and I, after years of architectural practice, am now as much writer as architect.

When Kevin called me again five years ago to ask if I'd like to write and illustrate a regular column for the magazine, I was delighted. I love to draw, and this gave me the opportunity to explain in hand-drawn images what I was describing in words. Executive Editor Charles Miller suggested the title "Drawing Board," and we were off and running.

Every two months I send off an essay, complete with illustrations; and a few weeks later, it arrives back on my doorstep within the bindings of *Fine Homebuilding*, just like magic. I know what hard work it is to put a magazine together—to move relentlessly from one issue deadline to the next. And I've had enough work published in other venues to appreciate that it's not always easy to maintain grace under fire. But these two guys (and I say "guys" because gentlemen just doesn't seem to fit these two ex-builders) along with the rest of the *Fine Homebuilding* crew, are always positive, always on top of the inevitable next issue, and always mindful of what information and inspiration their readership is looking for.

So I'd like to take this opportunity to thank all the staff at *Fine Homebuilding* for their dedication to serving the homeowners, builders, craftspeople, architects, and designers that depend on their insights and efforts, and bringing the best of American residential construction to us in every issue. Their role in improving the quality of this country's housing stock should not be underestimated. A huge thank you to all.

Contents

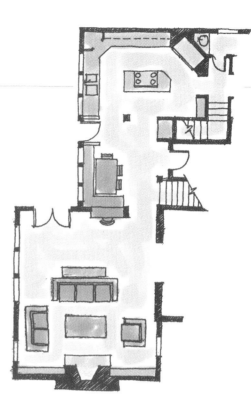

Foreword

When the success of Sarah Susanka's first book, *The Not So Big House*, thrust her into the national spotlight, she didn't waste much time basking in the attention. She hit the road. Sarah became an architectural missionary preaching the gospel of good design in the wilderness of residential construction, where architects are rare and looked upon with suspicion. Her message? Good design doesn't have to be expensive, doesn't have to mean a huge house, and doesn't require an advanced degree to understand it. She's not talking Architecture with a capital "A." If you can appreciate having a cup holder in your car, you can appreciate having a dedicated spot in your house for sorting the mail, with slots for bills, a trash can, and a recycling bin for all those catalogs.

Nearly five years ago, I asked Sarah to write a regular column on design for *Fine Homebuilding* magazine, but not just because she's a good architect. What makes Sarah special, besides her missionary zeal, is that she can write about residential design without referring to halls and stairs as "horizontal and vertical circulation corridors." But she does more than translate architectural jargon into plain English. She can explain why it's uncomfortable to be alone in a big room with tall ceilings, and why you're drawn to a cozy, light-filled window seat.

This book is a collection of 30 essays that Sarah originally wrote for *Fine Homebuilding*'s "Drawing Board" column. Whether you're building a new home or remodeling an old one, these not-so-big solutions will help you make a better place to live.

Kevin Ireton, Editor-in-Chief,
Fine Homebuilding

Introduction

Our homes have a lot more to them than meets the eye. Because we all live in them, we assume that we understand them, that we know how to design one, and that we know how to make it just right for ourselves and our loved ones. But our homes are, in fact, pretty complicated places, and it generally requires significant expertise to transform an idea into a workable reality, be it a small touch up or a full-fledged overhaul.

The following pages will help you understand your dwelling place in a completely new way. This book is a training manual for those who want to learn how to tailor their homes to fit their lifestyles. The insights and explanations come from many years of experience as a residential architect, working with normal, everyday folks, with normal everyday house problems…a bathroom where the door hits the toilet when opened all the way; an isolated, cramped kitchen; a house with no peaceful, quiet places to escape the noise and distraction of TVs, stereos, and computer games. These are real problems encountered daily by households across the globe, but they can all be easily solved if we simply rethink the way we approach space and function in our homes.

Each of these essays originally appeared in *Fine Homebuilding* magazine, where, for nearly five years, my column "Drawing Board" has appeared. In each essay, I've offered readers the opportunity to share in the know-how that comes from working on these everyday house headaches for a couple of decades. Your home's shortcomings almost certainly have characteristics and cures that are similar to someone else's. By sharing the solutions and the thought processes behind them, my hope is that we will gradually improve our housing stock, both existing and new.

It's exciting that these columns are now all collected into one volume, where they're more accessible to a larger audience. Since they appeared in a magazine initially, I wrote them one at a time, each a couple of months apart. It wasn't until I reread them in preparation for this book that I realized just how much useful and easy-to-implement advice they contain. Whatever your budget, there are ideas here that will help you make your home support rather than obstruct your daily routine.

I actually began the "Drawing Board" column just after I had completed my first book, *The Not So Big House: A Blueprint for the Way We Really Live*. Little did I know at the time that the book would strike such a chord with readers. Since its publication, a veritable movement has taken hold, comprising people who are tired of big, amorphous houses with little or no soul. The book explains in simple language what my architectural clients have been requesting for years—a house that's not so big but ultimately better. Better because it's a carefully crafted form of the inhabitants' personal expression and better because it's designed for today's lifestyle rather than that of a century ago. Its sequel, *Creating the Not So Big House: Insights and Ideas for the New American Home,* demonstrates how these concepts have been translated into actual homes.

As I traveled the country explaining the concepts behind building Not So Big, I realized there was a vast audience for this rather simple message—that we can do more with less space and actually have houses that feel bigger and work far better in the process. The *Fine Homebuilding* articles have given me an opportunity to elaborate on the topics in the books and help make them applicable for anyone trying to fine-tune their home to their way of life.

It's important to point out that none of the ideas that encompass this Not So Big approach to design is particularly new or revolutionary. Architects have been working with them since Frank Lloyd Wright introduced the concept of the Usonian House—a house for every man—in the mid-1930s. But what hasn't been available until now is a language with which homeowners, builders, realtors, interior designers, and architects can talk to each other about what makes a home work today and about what makes it

sing. This collection of essays offers simple concepts that will help further this goal.

I firmly believe that if we can simply explain to each other what we really want in and from our dwellings, we'll find answers that are less resource consumptive and far more satisfying to the soul. Our homes willingly reveal the secret to their metamorphis, but we have to learn how to pay attention and listen. Read on, and find out how to listen to your own dwelling place and how to transform it, regardless of its size, shape, or character, into the home of your dreams.

ONE

The House on Its Site

W hen most people contemplate building a new home, they assume that the first order of business is to choose or design a plan to build. But, in fact, the first step is always to find the site that you want to build on. When you work with an architect, you'll find that the design for the house or addition to an existing house is as much influenced by the opportunities and constraints of the site as it is by your particular functional and aesthetic desires. If you try to select a design before a site, you will almost certainly find that the design misses many or all of the potentials of the piece of land you ultimately choose.

This was eminently evident in one new house I saw a few years ago. The house was positioned on a hill, facing south overlooking a magnificent vista, but there was not a single window looking toward that extraordinary view. My guess is that the design had been picked out of a plan book long before the site had been chosen, and the original plan had been designed to be highly energy efficient with its blind face oriented to the north. This new house had the blind face oriented to the south—just the direction one wants lots of glass in most climates. It was so sad to see such an incredible view completely ignored because the house/site relationship had not been understood.

In this part you'll learn how to look at a piece of property, not only with respect to how it looks and feels but also in terms of what legal and physical constraints may be present and what hidden opportunities can be explored in the design for maximum benefit and livability. When a house is designed to take advantage of, and be integrated into, its natural environment, the result becomes far more than just another house. It seems to sing. It has a sense of harmony about it that's palpable.

You'll also learn how to tailor your house to the neighborhood, so that it fits into its surrounding context. You'll be able to see how decisions about exterior composition can affect the overall impression that the house gives to the street, to the neighborhood, and most importantly, to you.

Site Selection: Avoiding the Pitfalls

Discovering that you can't put your house where you want to put it on your own piece of property can come as a shock. You can avoid that shock by knowing what the constraints are before you buy. First, let's look at legal restrictions.

Legal constraints that affect siting

Setbacks are buffer zones around the borders of a piece of property that define exactly how close you can build to the property lines (drawing left). The more you build, the more you'll learn about how different municipalities interpret setback rules—they are all different. In most cities I have worked in, driveways are allowed in setback areas, but no structure. Even roof overhangs are prohibited from extending into the setback area in some cities. Before buying any lot, it's prudent to check with local officials about what portion of the lot can be covered with a building.

While you're inquiring about setbacks, you should also ask about easements. Easements are legal agreements granting use of a piece of land to someone other than the owner. For example, easements are often granted for driveways, power lines, or irrigation ditches. Easements can also cover intan-

Setbacks affect the buildable portion of a lot. Municipalities keep the building density down by requiring buffers, or setbacks, around a house. In this case, the house has to be 35 ft. back from the street, 30 ft. from the rear property line and 10 ft. from the side-yard boundaries.

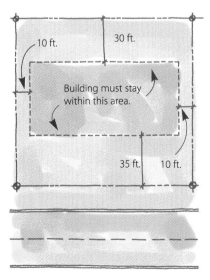

10 ft.

30 ft.

Building must stay within this area.

35 ft.   10 ft.

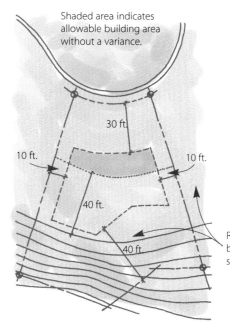

Shaded area indicates allowable building area without a variance.

30 ft.

10 ft.

10 ft.

40 ft.

40 ft.

Required building setbacks

Easements can further impinge on the buildable portion of a lot.
In addition to the setback requirements, this property was also subject to a scenic-river easement, requiring buildings to be 40 ft. back from the bluff line. This made the site unbuildable without a variance.

gible things, such as views or solar access. Although the seller of the property should inform you of any easements, it doesn't always happen. For example, one of my clients had to apply for a variance to build on a lot with a scenic easement (drawing top right).

When I evaluate potential sites with a client, I'm often looking for a lot that cost-effectively accepts the house they have in mind. If, for example, you're concerned about having the garage doors visible from the street, you need a lot with sufficient width for a driveway and turnaround to be located to the side or back of the house (drawing bottom right).

After the legal hurdles, check for the natural ones

Where wells and septic systems are needed, find out how much these two items are likely to add to the construction cost of the home, and make sure you include it in your construction budget.

Soils can be some of the most pesky and invisible problems to identify. Many architects will recommend that you obtain a soils test before starting the design of a new home. Unfortunately, this can be an expensive proposition, and many builders think that such a precaution is unnecessary. Soil problems that have not been identified until the start of construction, however, are

30 ft.

10 ft.

15 ft.

50 ft.

This city required that no driveways or roof overhangs extend beyond the required side setbacks.
A survey acquired before the start of design located existing trees and contours, which became features of the design for the house. A tuck-under garage required careful configuration, given the slope of the land.

Soil problems that have not been identified until the start of construction are responsible for a great number of financial difficulties. By the time the problems surface, the job is well under way, and the problems must be solved—whatever the cost.

responsible for a great number of financial difficulties. By the time the problems surface, the job is well under way, and the problems must be solved—whatever the cost. I recall one such situation, the first house I designed in Minnesota. My clients had purchased a lot for a surprisingly good price. Once the excavator started to dig, we found out why: The lot had a bog under one corner of the house. The soggy, organic material wouldn't support a standard foundation, requiring $20,000 worth of pilings.

When I am working with a client, I ask local officials, builders, neighbors, and surveyors familiar with the area if there has been any history of soil problems. If the answer is yes, I recommend a soils test. If the client declines to have one made, I suggest putting aside a contingency budget. The problem is a tricky one, though, because until the soils problem is identified, it is difficult to guess how much it will cost to remedy.

In developments, the building area can be constrained where engineered fill for a building pad has been located. If you want to build beyond this pad, you may need to invest in more engineered fill to give your house a sturdy base.

Turn drawbacks into advantages

In the northern parts of the country, foundations get expensive because the frost footings have to extend at least 4 ft. below the ground. This makes basement space relatively inexpensive. After all, a 4-ft. deep excavation is already halfway there (drawing facing page, top left). For this reason, in cold climates the least expensive house form is one in which the lower level is used for living space. Finding a site with a slope that allows the rear side of the lower level to have good-size windows (preferably facing south) can make this living space as appealing as main-level space (drawing facing page, top right). If the slope is too great, however, the benefit is lost because additional foundation work is required to support the lower-level floor space.

In the Northern Hemisphere, look for south-facing lot

The ideal orientation for a house in the Northern Hemisphere is to have its long face looking south. So a site that offers good views to the south with access from another direction is usually best. Having the long

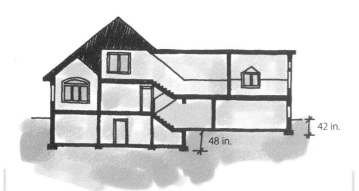

Keep digging.
In cold climates, you have to bury the footings several feet to keep them below the frost line. In this house, digging another 4 ft. gained a full basement.

Sometimes a sloping lot can be a benefit.
A basement room doesn't feel at all like a basement if you include full-height windows to brighten the space.

side of the house facing south allows you to control the sunlight much more easily than if the long side faces east and west (drawing bottom right).

Easterly and westerly sunlight falls on a house when the sun is lower in the sky, making the sunlight difficult to filter. This situation usually isn't a problem in the winter, but in the summer it can cause tremendous heat gain.

South light, on the other hand, is high in the sky in the summer; overhangs and exterior trellises can keep sunlight from entering the house. In the winter, when sunlight is welcome inside, the southern sun angle is lower and penetrates below the overhangs.

What if you can't find the perfect site for your house? The answer, of course, is creative compromise. If, for example, you have a lot with great views to the north, you may want to include some high-on-the-wall south-facing windows to bring daylight into the house.

No matter how big or small the house you are planning, finding a lot that allows you to build the house of your dreams requires some amount of research up front. Checking on legal and site constraints before signing a purchase agreement can help you avoid some expensive pitfalls, keep construction costs down, and make the resulting house a better place in which to live.

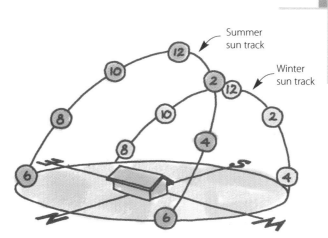

The southern sun is easier to control.
In the Northern Hemisphere, it's best to orient a house with the long side facing south, where wide overhangs can keep out the high summer sun.

Selecting a Site for a New Home

Whenever I sit down with new clients to discuss the design of a new home, the conversation frequently begins with this question: "Which comes first? House plan or lot selection?"

Architects will give you one unequivocal answer: lot first, house plan second. A home is really the combination of both the house and the land on which it is placed. If the two are awkwardly matched, no matter what you do, that house will not easily be made to feel like a home.

If you train yourself to think beyond the obvious, you can often find some really good deals when it comes to lot selection.

I think of a house I saw while working with some clients in the mountains of Colorado. Their site was extraordinary, straddling a ridge, with panoramic views available no matter where we sited the house. I advised that rather than place the house right on top of the ridge, we nestle it down, essentially making one side partially earth sheltered so that the house would settle into its site (drawing facing page, bottom). By doing so, the roofs would continue the natural slopes of the surrounding terrain.

They agreed with this advice, having seen what happens when you try to compete with nature. They took me to see a neighboring property where a house was just being completed. What they showed me was horrifying. On a site at least as precipitous as theirs, right on top of the ridge sat a large brick Federalist Colonial house (drawing facing page, top left). We were looking at it from the bottom of the driveway and were at least 50 ft. below it. It looked like a jail. Had this house been placed on a residential street in New England, it would have looked in its element (drawing facing page, top right). In the majesty of a mountainous wilderness, it

seemed to be thumbing its nose at Mother Nature, trying to be higher and more majestic than what surrounded it. Instead, it looked ridiculous.

This example is extreme, but it illustrates why the lot must come first. If, like my clients, these new homeowners had listened to their site, taking their cues for design from the surrounding views, the sun, the vegetation, and the fabric and contours of the land, they could have had a truly extraordinary house. My guess is that they had the house plan picked out long before they selected the site, and it hadn't occurred to them that the two might not be a good combination.

Even if you have a favorite plan that you've always wanted to build when you can afford it, try not to get so married to it that you can't let it be modified to take advantage of the opportunities presented by the site.

Don't build right on the ridge.
If you've got a site that straddles a ridge line, nestle the house into the ground on one side or another. Rooflines that echo the slope of the hill will help wed the house to the land.

Better yet, recognize what it is about the plan that appeals to you, and when you have purchased land, design a house that includes the features of the plan that you like and integrates them with the features of the lot.

Architects are frequently uncomfortable when a house they've designed for one site gets built on another site with different characteristics. For example, imagine a passive-solar house with most of its windows facing south and with a concrete floor for thermal storage. If this house is instead built so that its windows face north, the house, far from being a model of energy efficiency, is now hard to keep comfortable in the winter months because of the heat loss through the north-facing glass.

Evaluating two sites by a small lake.
In this small development, Lot 1 cost $10,000 more than Lot 2.

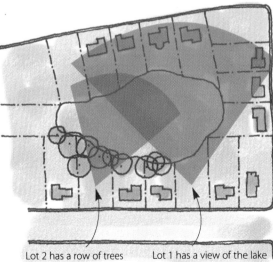

Lot 2 has a row of trees limiting the view of the lake.

Lot 1 has a view of the lake and the houses beyond.

Identify a site's characteristics

When assessing a potential building site, the first thing to do is to identify both the liabilities and the opportunities it offers. Every lot has both obvious and hidden characteristics. In a residential neighborhood, for example, the most obvious characteristics may be the locations and styles of neighboring houses. You may need to give careful thought to how windows in your new house might be located to minimize loss of privacy for yourself and your neighbors. Perhaps there is a good-size tree in the backyard that could provide opportunities for some special views from inside the house. Or perhaps a neighbor is an avid gardener with a yard that might provide a colorful backdrop for much of the year. Noting the locations of these features and designing the house to take advantage of them can greatly enhance the livability of a home.

In new developments with larger lots, the location of each house is not predetermined. In this case, people are often surprised and upset when a neighbor's house springs up right in line with a treasured view.

When I am helping a client design a new home in such a development, we find out where neighbors are planning to place their houses. If the adjacent lots are still unsold, we try to predict building locations for future houses and plan the client's house accordingly.

Get the architect involved before you buy a building site

If you are planning to work with an architect to design your home, consider letting the architect help you to pick the site as well. When you have two or three lot options to choose from, your architect may be able to shed some light on the benefits of one over another.

For example, I once saved clients $10,000 with a single one-hour site visit (How's that for return on investment?). They were considering two different sites in a new development of half-acre lots (drawing facing page). The more expensive one had an unobstructed view to hills across a small lake. Unfortunately, the hills were sprinkled with rather plain tract houses. But it was a long view nonetheless, and the lake was picturesque. The other site was only three lots away, but a stand of trees obstructed the view to the lake and hills beyond. Although the trees would provide a pleasant view from the living

spaces of the house, the couple really wanted to be able to see the lake, so they were leaning toward the first lot.

When I looked at the two, I realized that with some judicious pruning of the lower branches of the trees on the second lot, they would be able to get the desired view to the lake and also keep the house-sprinkled hills hidden from sight (drawing above). My clients were delighted with the suggestion. They purchased the lot with the tree buffer and built a home that took advantage of both the sheltering presence of the trees and the longer view to the lake.

This is the kind of thinking that allows you to find opportunities that aren't immediately apparent. If you train yourself to think beyond the obvious, you can often find some really good deals when it comes to lot selection. So find the land first. Then work on either finding, modifying, or designing a house that will blend comfortably with its site, using the opportunities it presents to add to the home's personality.

The trees allowed the view to be tailored.
With careful pruning of trees, the view from Lot 2 takes in the lake while screening out the houses on the opposite shore, giving the lot a better view than its more expensive neighbor.

Composing the Exterior of the House

Many new homes look as though they had been designed from the sidewalk in front of the house. If you stand there, it generally looks as though someone paid attention to whether windows align and how rooflines interact with one another (drawing facing page). But walk around the house, and you are likely to see that nothing on a side elevation has been given any thought at all. Windows are scattered willy-nilly across the surface. Roofs are sheared off indiscriminately, and brick and stone veneers stop abruptly at the edges of the front facade, leaving no doubt that this beauty is only skin deep (drawing facing page). The side and rear elevations of this house bear no relationship to the front and have no discernible composition. Window locations have been determined solely by the needs of the interior.

It is extremely rare that you view a house from straight on, so the beauty of the front elevation is almost never experienced. We are building houses as though they were perceived two-dimensionally when, of course, we live in a three-dimensional world.

Older homes have integrated exteriors

If you look at a house built 70 years ago or more, you'll see a sense of integrity. All its sides are recognizably part of a single composition (drawings p. 19). The sides and back of the house bear the same stylistic influences as the front, even in modest homes.

We are building houses as though they were perceived two-dimensionally when, of course, we live in a three-dimensional world.

Then something happened around the 1940s, perhaps as a result of the postwar construction boom. With simply constructed houses built closely together, the side and rear elevations were hardly seen. In an effort to save time and money, designers and builders restricted any special detailing to the face of the house that could be seen from the street.

Jump to the end of the twentieth century. You'll find that most new houses are more complex forms, and lot sizes have increased, making the sides of a home more visible. There are more bumps and corners in the front facade, and the rooflines are typically many and varied. The brick detailing, however, still happens only to the walls that face the street. I call this design brick tape because it is so obviously pasted on.

In addition, most of these new homes have few windows on their side elevations—presumably to minimize the presence of any neighbors. The facade is exactly that: a facade ineffectively disguising an amazing lack of thought about composition.

Get back to thinking in three dimensions

What's the solution? With the increased use of computer-aided design (CAD), it will become more typical to view houses in three dimensions before they are built. But until this becomes the norm, home buyers need to become more savvy about what to ask for or look for on side and rear elevations to ensure that their new home will have a sense of integrity. Looking at the plan of the subject house, you can see that brick is shown only on the street-facing parts of the front facade (drawing p. 18, top). For the brick to look like a real brick base—and not brick tape—it needs to continue all the way around the bumps and indents of the street face, and to extend for at least a few feet down the side of the house (drawing p. 18, bottom). The more that you can wrap the same materials

Houses aren't viewed just from the front.
Believe it or not, these elevations are of the same house. Clearly, all the design effort went into the front facade. We seem to have forgotten that houses are often seen from the side. On a corner lot, the location of this house, side and rear elevations are as visible as the front. They all need to be considered equally.

Extending horizontal lines improves the situation.
By adding windows, a bit of brickwork, and a continuous trim line aligning with the top of the brick, the house begins to look as though the adjacent elevations were related to one another.

Wrap the detail around the house.
Better yet, extend the materials and stylistic characteristics around the entire house for greatest integrity.

future buyers than one with its personality apparent only from straight on. And it is more likely to please its original owners.

Consider window placement

Notice how the addition of windows to the side of a house gives it a much more engaging and three-dimensional appeal. There is, of course, the additional benefit of light entering on two sides of the rooms. For me, this increased daylight outweighs any fear of the occasional glimpse of a neighbor. Windows should be considered from both sides of the wall. Promoting views and gathering daylight are certainly important, but the placement of the windows on the exterior is critical to a house's exterior composition.

One of the reasons the classic colonial home is still so popular is that it has a clear, straightforward composition (drawing facing page, bottom left). Windows are located symmetrically, usually in equally spaced increments, aligned with windows above and below. Although this may seem formal, colonial symmetry clearly has more appeal than the randomly scattered windows found on most side and rear facades today.

When designing a house, rather than plunking each window in the center of each room and letting it fall where it may on the exterior, give some thought to alignment. Make windows on adjacent floors relate to

around the sides of the house, the more solid and well composed the house ultimately will look (drawing above).

For most people, the decision to wrap the front-facing materials around the house comes down to expense. Often, in an effort to save money initially, the long-term value of the home is dramatically compromised. A house with a personality that extends around and through it will hold greater appeal to

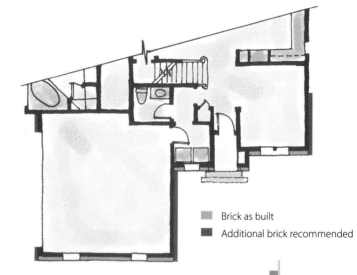

Brick as built

Additional brick recommended

each other in some way. Perhaps they can be the same width as one another, with their jambs aligned. Or perhaps like text on a page, they can be aligned on just one side as in the bottom drawing on the facing page. In many ways this composition of the exterior is an exercise in graphic design. You are aiming to make the facade look pleasing to the eye and also to have some relationship to the other elevations of the house

When I am designing a house, I will often develop a graphic theme with respect to windows. For example, I may use sets of three windows in most rooms and then extend this to five in the main living space. A good architect or designer will be able to balance interior light and view needs with exterior compositional needs and arrive at a design that has a beauty that extends all the way through the house.

Although the end result of thinking about the house as a single composition is clearly superior to a house not given such attention, much of the added cost comes in paying someone to think through the design. Few people ask for this added design consideration, and so it rarely happens; but it's not hard to do. If more people were to ask for this additional service, the quality and appearance of our suburbs and new developments would improve dramatically. Good design takes more time, but it's worth it.

Veneer extensions can help. Wrapping the brick or stone around the corners for a portion of the sidewalls will give a house some integrity.

They used to get it right. Older homes such as this colonial (left) and Craftsman (right) typically have continuity of character on all sides.

How Roofs—and Now Roof Trusses —Influence the Look of a House

When you look at houses in your neighborhood, do you notice their roofs? Do you know the difference between a 3-in-12 and an 8-in-12 slope? Do you know how roof slope affects the look of the house? If you're not sure what these questions even refer to but you're curious, read on.

There is a nostalgia for the old roof forms, such as the bungalow or Cape, that say "I am a house" so clearly.

The roof gives us our first style clue

The diagrams on the facing page illustrate three different styles of house. The first, a Prairie-style house, has a relatively low roof slope of 4-in-12. The second house, a Colonial saltbox, has a significantly steeper slope of 12-in-12. And the third house, a Gothic Revival, has an even steeper slope of 17-in-12. Even without any detail to describe the character of these houses, your eye picks up the general style of each one.

Where did this system of slope designation come from? It refers to the measuring system that carpenters have traditionally used to lay out and cut roof rafters. The x-in-12 ratio told the carpenter that for every 12 in. of run—the horizontal distance covered by the rafter—the rafter would rise a certain number of inches (drawing facing page, bottom).

Prairie style

Colonial saltbox

Gothic Revival

Once understood, this ratio gives us an immediate visual image of the roof slope.

But this traditional designation came from an era when time was cheap and rafters were cut and raised individually. Nowadays, roofs are more typically fabricated off site in a truss factory to save on the labor of a hand-cut roof. The trusses are then trucked to the site, where they are lifted into place with a crane.

Truss fabrication has made roof construction more affordable than it used to be, but it has also made some of the most cost-effective roof-cum-room forms of the past much less economical to create. The economy of the prefabricated truss comes in large part from its ability to minimize bearing walls by transferring loads to the outside walls of the house.

Trusses do this with a multitude of web members—the diagonal braces that connect the chords of the truss together (drawing p. 22, top left). Unfortunately, these webs make the area within the roof unusable as living space unlike the trusses in many old houses, such as a Cape with a 10-in-12 roof or a French Colonial with a 12-in-12 roof, which can accommodate living space in the attic.

There is a partial solution to this problem. You can build the roof with attic-storage trusses, which have webs configured to keep a portion of the attic open (drawing p. 22, bottom). But they are more expensive than standard trusses, and they still don't provide as much interior living space as their hand-framed counterpart.

The paradox of truss-built roofs

There is a nostalgia for the old roof forms, such as the bungalow or Cape, that say "I am a house" so clearly. Many people love the look of such a home, with its dormers and its cottage charm. Others like the feel of the rooms created within, with their cozy sloped ceilings, window alcoves, and nooks and crannies. But sadly, the economical roof-construction techniques of today have actually made these economical houses of yesterday more expensive to build than their standard, two-story, truss-roofed offspring.

Roofs have a powerful role in determining the style of a house.
Even without the signature details that will enrich these houses, their character is conveyed by their roofs. The low-slope hip roof of the house on the left signals that it is a Prairie-style house. The steep, clipped-off roof in the center says Colonial saltbox. The steeper-yet roof on the right announces a Gothic Revival house.

Roof-slope designations relate to the framing square. Carpenters describe the slope of a roof with a ratio that tells the number of inches that a rafter rises for each 12 in. that it spans horizontally. This example shows the slope of a 9-in-12 roof (also written 9:12).

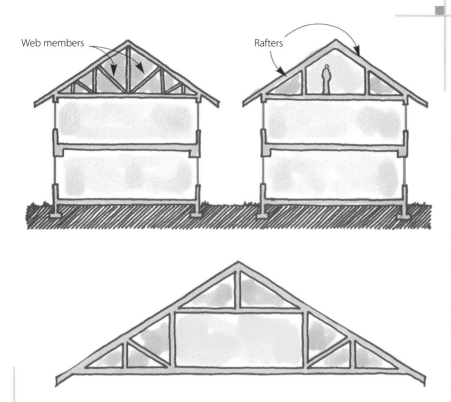

Web members

Rafters

A truss roof compared to a roof framed with rafters.
In a typical truss roof (below left), the webs render the attic uninhabitable. If the ridge is high enough, however, a roof framed with rafters can allow a room.

An attic truss.
Attic trusses create a cavity between the webs for a room.

and dormers in these broad expanses of wall and roof that conceal the truss space (drawings facing page), we suddenly warm to the image.

What's going on here? We are creatures of habit. We know what a house is supposed to look like, and we know that the space where the trusses reside is supposed to be lived in. The addition of windows makes us believe that the roof is lived in, even if it's actually a forest of truss webs.

Take advantage of trusses while minimizing the impact of the garage

Truss technology allows the entire 30-ft. width of a three-car garage to be spanned without bearing walls (drawing facing page, top). This provides a great convenience for the homeowner. There are no columns or critical walls to smack with your car, and it's cheap to build.

But if the roof slope is steep, the roof over this garage gets truly enormous. Notice what happens, however, if we turn the garage footprint 90° and locate the doors on the side. The dimension of the garage facing the street is reduced to 24 ft. The roof gets lower, and the facade can be decorated with windows in place of those massive doors (drawing bottom right).

This is one of the reasons that houses today look bigger. The roof typically sits above all the living space, rather than incorporating some of it. In an attempt to mimic older house forms, you will often see new homes with these same roof shapes and dormers, but when you get inside, you discover that the dormers are just there for show.

Because the roof contains no living space, the footprint of the house has to increase to accommodate the same square footage on the main level.

I often hear people bemoaning the proportions of new homes. The garages look so dominant, the roofs so massive. But here's something interesting: If we add windows

Toward balancing proportion and technology

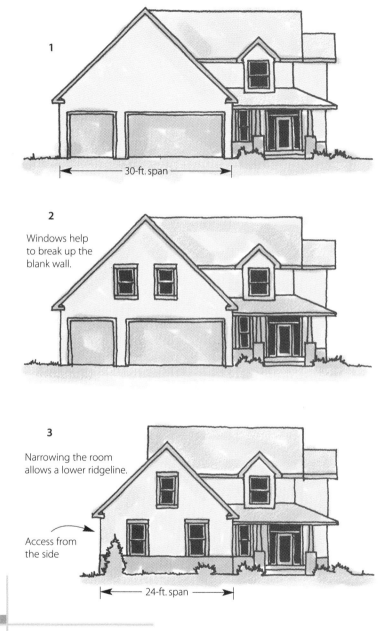

So what's the solution to making contemporary homes look better proportioned? The most important thing to remember is that just because we have the technology to build big, it doesn't necessarily produce the most aesthetically pleasing results.

Many architects and designers still design houses with rooms in the roof space even though it's more expensive. And many will try to downplay the garage in other ways, such as locating doors so that they are not visible from the street. The end result is a house that looks less massive and has some of the old-world charm that so many people today are seeking.

Make sure your house says a little something about your priorities and your personality. If you want a house that announces to the world that your cars are more important to you than anything else, by all means make the garage roof big.

But if you'd rather invite your family and friends into a house that provides a comfortable respite, scale down a bit. It's all related to roof slope and how that roof is made. Spending a little more on design and a little less on sheer volume can make a huge difference in the way a new home both looks and feels.

1 ← 30-ft. span →

2 Windows help to break up the blank wall.

3 Narrowing the room allows a lower ridgeline.

Access from the side

← 24-ft. span →

Toning down the garage.
Roof trusses can create impressive clear spans, such as the 30 ft. required for this garage. But if the garage roof is steep, its unrelieved gable wall can dominate the house (1). Adding windows to the gable end helps to relate the garage to the rest of the house (2). An even better solution is to turn the garage footprint 90° and make the access from the side (3).

The Garage/House Connection

Look at most house plans today, and you'll find the garage, an ever more-massive affair, attached to the side of the house with garage doors facing the street and the door between the garage and the house entering into a utility room of some sort, often the laundry room. From the exterior, the garage's scale broadcasts the importance of the automobile in the homeowners' lives, while from the interior, the unceremonious entry commingles residents with dirty laundry and cleaning products.

Because most people come and go from their homes primarily through the garage, the door to the house should be in a place that reminds you of why you selected this particular building lot and this place to live.

Far from feeling welcomed, we return home to an assault on the senses. Surely there's a better way.

When a house has an attached three-car garage that elongates the house by 30 ft. to 36 ft., the whole composition can look more like a forbidding fortress than a home. There are a number of options to solve this problem. Although they are a little more expensive than the basic attached garage, they can make an enormous difference to the street image of the home.

A detached garage can be more interesting

In climates where snow and rain are not a frequent concern, a detached garage is an excellent solution to reducing the visual scale of the house. In many older homes, the walk from the garage to the house is a well-landscaped, beautiful transition from public to private realms. There's no rule that a new house can't do the same. It's simply convention that has eliminated the detached option. By locating the garage either behind the house or adjacent but some feet apart,

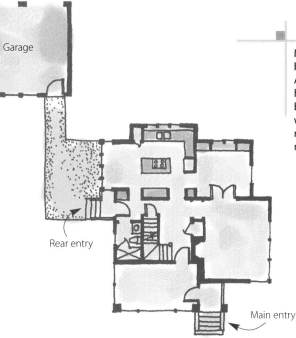

Garage

Rear entry

Main entry

there is greater spatial complexity and more interesting views from the street for the passerby and for you upon returning home (drawing right).

A breezeway keeps the rain off

In more inclement regions, the same strategy can be used, provided a sheltering roof canopy connects house and garage. This breezeway connection can be screened or windowed, or it can simply be a covered walkway. The connecting roof indicates that you have in effect entered the house, but you are still strongly connected with both front and back yards. If this space between house and garage can also be used to frame a view to the garden beyond, the approach to the house can be transformed into a truly delightful experience (drawing p. 26, top).

Garage doors don't have to face the street

Depending on site constraints, if the garage can be attached but turned 45° or 90° to the rest of the house, the result is an apparent reduction in scale. The garage doors are no longer lined up along the street face, and the driveway becomes more like a courtyard than a strip of asphalt connecting house and street (drawing p. 26, bottom).

This strategy has become popular in many upscale housing developments nationwide primarily because it de-emphasizes the garage and makes the houses look more like their traditional counterparts from the turn of the last century. It can, however, present some acoustical and air-quality challenges within the house because the garage shares at least two party walls and often a ceiling surface with the rest of the house. When there's nothing but a connecting door between house and garage, exhaust fumes can enter the house more easily. My suggestion is to always include an air-to-air heat exchanger in any new home, which ensures frequent air changes.

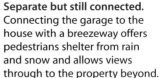

Separate but still connected. Connecting the garage to the house with a breezeway offers pedestrians shelter from rain and snow and allows views through to the property beyond.

Main entry

Garage

Angles create interest. Turning the garage at a 45° angle helps break up the facade of a house and creates the sense of an entry courtyard.

Where should you put the door between the house and the garage?

Because most people come and go from their homes primarily through the garage, the door to the house should be in a place that reminds you of why you selected this particular building lot and this place to live. If from the door you can see through to a view of the backyard, for example, your experience of returning home will be far more pleasant than if you are confronted with a view of the washer and dryer.

There are a number of other issues, however, that can help you determine the most appropriate location for your own situation. Families with children, for example, will have different concerns than a single person. A couple that shops frequently at Sam's Club will have different needs than someone who prefers to shop daily at the corner grocery store.

Here are some considerations to take into account as you determine the best location for your home:

Mudroom. If you live in a cold or wet climate, a mudroom close to the garage door is a great asset. Muddy shoes and wet outer garments can be removed before the mess is tracked through the house. The mudroom can also be a handy place to dispense with purses, briefcases, keys, etc. If these items are always placed at the most frequent entry point, they're less likely to be misplaced as well.

Mail-sorting place. If you typically pick up the mail on the way into the garage, then a place to set and sort that mail, close to the door, is a significant improvement over the alternative. Most people arrive back at the house, arms filled, and take all their booty, mail included, into the kitchen or dining room, where it frequently languishes on the island, peninsula, or dining-room table for days.

Garage

Main entry

Hide the doors to the side.
A favorite strategy today is to
obscure the garage by building
it into the mass of the house
with doors facing to the side.

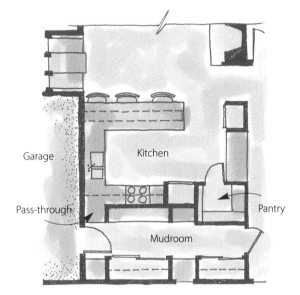

Garage

Kitchen

Pass-through

Pantry

Mudroom

A pass-through can ease
the grocery load.
Because it's a circuitous
walk from the garage to
the kitchen in this house,
a counter-height pass-
through offers a conven-
ient place to drop off
grocery bags.

Powder room. With small children, the
first order of business is often a mad dash to
the bathroom. Placing a bathroom close to
the back door can make that mad dash easier
for everyone. A bathroom may also serve
well in this location for children's comings
and goings while they play outside.

Kitchen or pantry. If you generally bring
groceries in through the garage and carry
them into the kitchen for unpacking, then it
makes sense to locate the garage and pantry
relatively close to one another.

An option that often makes the plan layout
a little simpler is a pass-through from a mudroom entry to the kitchen counter (drawing
above right).

A final word about the location of the
garage/house connection. Make sure there is
some sense of transition between the typically
gray, messy feel of the garage and the more
elegantly appointed quality of the home's interior living spaces. It's uncomfortable to be
thrust from one type of environment into another without preparation. As with a foyer at
the front door, a transition space from garage
to house gives both the time and the place to
change from public persona to private, and a
house that allows you to do this at the entry
you use every day is one that you'll love to
come home to.

TWO

Rethinking
Living Spaces

Whether remodeling or building new, with a little thought given to the routines and activities you actually engage in every day, you can either omit or better utilize a significant amount of space that is normally taken for granted as necessary in a house. By rethinking how you use each space, you can create a house that simultaneously functions better; is more efficient, more beautiful, and more spacious; and yet is often surprisingly smaller than you thought you needed.

Homeowners across the country have told me that after rethinking their rooms and the way they use them, they've realized that they have far more area available for reallocation than they'd ever realized. Rather than adding on or moving, they've been able to redistribute furnishings and functions to make the same amount of space accommodate many more activities.

The trick is to forget everything you think you know about how each space in the house is supposed to be. Instead of taking as gospel the way we normally furnish or layout a particular type of room, we can make each space take on more functions and actually work better in the process by listing the activities, furniture, or articles to be accommodated and tailoring the available space to those particular needs.

Instead of the current trend to build or add on a new room for every new activity, like a media room and an exercise room, for example, a house will feel more integrated and hospitable to its residents if there's more interaction between activity areas. This is true whether you are designing the main living areas of the house, which for most households include the kitchen and family room, or whether you are thinking about the process of entering the house, either as a guest or as a family member.

By connecting views from one place to another and by making places for each activity that are perfectly tailored to that activity's specific requirements, you'll find the house feels substantially bigger than it really is.

Designing a Gracious Entry

Have you noticed how few entries really greet visitors? Typically, when we think about the entry to a home, the front door comes to mind, and perhaps the foyer. But we rarely consider the experience of arrival at that doorway or what effect the process of moving from outside to inside might have on our guests.

In many older homes, where no provision was made for a foyer, or entry vestibule, it can be really awkward arranging furniture to allow space near the door for welcoming guests. The key is to think of entry as a process, not a thing. A good entry is a sequence of places, not simply a door.

To understand this better, imagine that you are walking up to a house with a poorly designed entry. You leave the sidewalk and make your way along a narrow concrete path toward the front door (drawing below). The five steps that raise you from the concrete path to door height have no landing at the top, so you have to perch on the top step while you wait to be greeted.

You push the doorbell button, but you can't hear its ring. So you're not certain that you have communicated your arrival. Because it is raining and there is no canopy over the door to protect you, you knock on the door to make sure that someone inside knows that you have arrived. With no window in the

This entry will leave you standing in the rain.
A roofless stoop doesn't do much to make visitors feel welcome.

Sidelites

Enlarged landing sheltered by roof overhang

Entry trellis

Transitional courtyard

A trellis and deep eaves improve the situation. An arched trellis at the sidewalk elegantly signals the change from the public world to that of the house. Extended roof eaves now provide some shelter at the door.

door to give you an indication of whether anyone is coming to your rescue, you knock again. The exterior of this house gives you no clue about what to expect inside. You already feel unwelcome.

You're about to leave when the door suddenly opens, and you're invited inside. Taking a single step through the door, you find yourself standing in the middle of the living room on a light-colored carpet. Now you are painfully aware of the mud on your shoes and the drips from your coat. Two children are squabbling just feet away from you, and the TV's noise fills the room. Embarrassment is the natural response unless you are on fairly intimate terms with the family. You want to apologize, turn around and leave as quickly as possible, and not inconvenience the members of this family any further.

What happened here?

In stepping through the door, which in this instance was the only gesture acknowledging that entering happens here, you left a situation where you were being drenched by rain, and you were suddenly an alien in the midst of someone's private realm. Without

windows to give you a view of the interior, you had no way to shape expectations about the inside of the house. There was no transition at all—no place to stand so that you wouldn't drip on the carpet, no place to switch gears and transform from the public persona that we all have for walking around town to the much more private persona that we use for meeting friends and family.

A gracious entry starts at the street

Now let's take this same example and remodel it into an entry that works. We'll start way back at the sidewalk, before we even enter the front yard. Over the path connecting street and house, we will place a trellis with roses or vines (drawing above). As you pass under this arbor, you know already that you have entered the territory of the house. The first transition has been made, and you no longer belong to the street. The archway is a welcoming gesture that says your presence will not be an imposition.

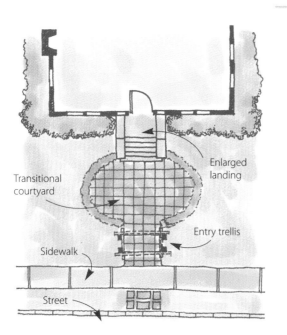

Transitional courtyard

Enlarged landing

Entry trellis

Sidewalk

Street

The remodeled-entry plan. A diminutive courtyard enhances the space between the entry trellis and the enlarged landing at the top of the steps.

In front of the steps, we will widen the pathway a little, maybe change the surface material or create a pattern in the surface, to give a psychological resting place before committing entirely to summoning the inhabitants. We'll also modify the steps to the front door, pulling them away from the door to allow at least a 3-ft. deep landing (drawing above). A deeper roof overhang will protect you from rain, and we'll flank the steps with low walls wide enough for flowerpots.

Now, as you move toward the door, you feel accepted by the house, offered a waiting

The key is to think of entry as a process, not a thing. A good entry is a sequence of places, not simply a door.

place that is pleasant to stand in and that gives shelter from the elements and from the street. As you ring the doorbell, you can hear the ring, letting you know that communication has occurred.

On both sides of the door, we will add small sidelites, perhaps with beveled glass, so that you can see that someone is coming to answer the door. The sidelites don't have to be big windows to the heart of the house. Just a minimal visual connection between interior and exterior makes an enormous difference to the graciousness of the entry process.

The entry continues inside

Believe it or not, you can take a few square feet off a living room for an entry and make the living room feel larger. The drawings on the facing page illustrate how. In the original scheme, the door opened into a corner of the living room at the base of the stair.

In the remodeled room, you are welcomed into a vestibule that was created by taking a small area of the living room and separating it with an archway and a change of flooring. Although not large, it offers that final transitional place in an entry sequence—the place to take off your wet coat and muddy shoes, the place to settle into the "friends and family"

No distinction between living
room and entry

Remodeled entry provides a transition
zone before entering the living room.

persona before stepping into the occupants'
living room.

Although square footage has been taken
away from the living room for the entry
vestibule, the room feels bigger and less
awkward because both the living room and
the vestibule now have their own designated
areas. Square footage alone is not an accurate
gauge of how big a room feels or how well it
functions.

Use a checklist to avoid omissions

A well-designed entry provides a gradual
transition from the outdoors to the
indoors, with attention paid to visitors at
every turn. When you're designing an entry,
consider using the following set of questions
to evaluate the design you're working on:

- Can visitors see where the entry is as
  they approach the house?

- Is there an indication that you're within the territory of the house before you
  have reached the door?

- Is there a place to stand out of the elements at the door?

- Is the doorbell easily found?

- Can visitors hear the doorbell?

- Is there a glass area for visitors to see if
  anyone is coming to the door?

- Once the door has been opened and
  the visitors have been accepted into the
  house, is there a place for them to
  stand, to take off their coats, and to
  adjust to being inside before they step
  into the living spaces of the house?

Solving these issues can transform a cold
and unfriendly house into a welcoming one.
The experience of entering a home is crucial
to how comfortable it will feel to your
friends and neighbors, and probably even to
yourself.

**On the inside, the entry
needs a transition, too.**
An archway extension of the
stairway wall in this house
created a transition zone
between the front door and
the living room without taking up a lot of space. The
change in floor covering
emphasizes the separation.

Mudroom Design

Growing up in England, I always enjoyed visiting the homes of friends who lived on country estates. Their houses were rich with features that my own family's conventional small house lacked. Of particular fascination were the mudrooms, which seemed to me, at the age of 10, a marvelous invention because they miraculously eliminated adult concerns over the comings and goings of children.

England is lush and green because it rains a lot. The countryside turns into a muddy wonderland—delightful for children and pets, but a constant burden to parents trying to keep a tidy house. In particular, one friend's home, a farmhouse that was at least 100 years old, had a mudroom that has

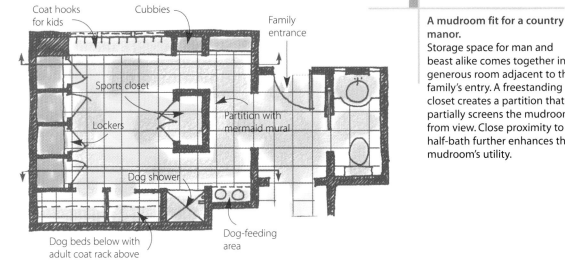

Coat hooks for kids
Cubbies
Family entrance
Sports closet
Lockers
Partition with mermaid mural
Dog shower
Dog beds below with adult coat rack above
Dog-feeding area

A mudroom fit for a country manor.
Storage space for man and beast alike comes together in a generous room adjacent to the family's entry. A freestanding closet creates a partition that partially screens the mudroom from view. Close proximity to a half-bath further enhances the mudroom's utility.

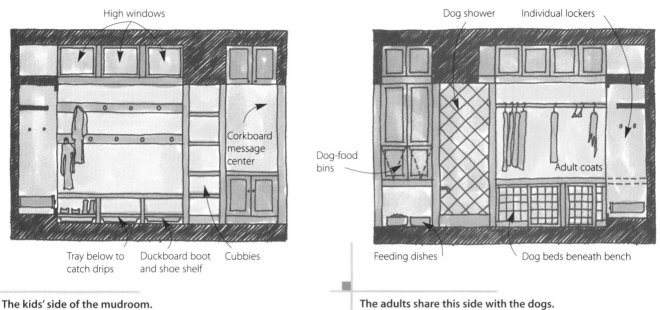

The kids' side of the mudroom.
Coat hooks at two levels accommodate kids of all ages.
Muddy boots are stored on duckboards over trays strate-
gically placed to catch their drips. High windows let in
light without stealing valuable wall space.

The adults share this side with the dogs.
With its tile floor and close connection to the entry, the
mudroom is a perfect place to feed, house, and bathe the
dogs. A closet pole above the dogs' bedding provides
space for adult coats and jackets.

influenced me greatly in my residential-
architecture practice (drawings above and
facing page). This mudroom's scale and features seemed ideal for its purpose of control-
ling mud, storing outdoor clothing and
footwear, and providing a home for a pair of
unruly dogs. Out of sight but with immediate access from the back door, it actually
made changing into and out of outdoor gear
fun. If you live in a rainy or snowy climate, a
mudroom such as this one is a parents'
dream. Here's what I learned from it, along
with some variations for smaller spaces. I've
also included a list of mudroom features and
considerations that will help you design a
mudroom with maximum usefulness.

- Proximity to traffic flow
- Intriguing entry to entice kids to use it
- Pegs at kid height
- Shoe storage
- Drip area for wet footwear
- Cubbies for purses, backpacks, mittens,
  hats, etc.
- Lockers for family members
- Hanging area for adults' coats
- Pet area
- Sports equipment storage

Location is crucial

Whenever you're designing for children, it's critical to remember that if
something isn't really obvious and in the
line of motion, it won't get used. A mudroom down the hall, third door on the right,
is simply not going to work without some

A mudroom down the hall, third door on the right, is simply not going to work....The first rule is to put the mudroom in a convenient spot.

heavy-handed enforcement. So the first rule is to put the mudroom in a convenient spot. And if you can make the space intriguing, you're almost guaranteed cooperation by the younger set.

The entrance to my friend's mudroom, just to the right of the back door, had its separating wall set back a bit from the hallway, so that you'd already stepped through the wall membrane before you entered the mudroom proper. This feature alone would probably have been sufficient to invite further exploration. But in addition, the wall was painted a deep royal blue with a mural of a mermaid on it. This painting had the effect of engaging kids in the experience of moving into a new world.

Although most mudrooms don't include a mermaid attendant, the concepts used here can be employed in a mudroom of almost any size. If you place the mudroom doorway next to the most frequently used entrance to the house so that it can be seen without its entire contents being displayed, and if you make the doorway something a little out of the ordinary—maybe with an arched top or with trim work that's painted an unusual color—you'll have accomplished the most important function of the room: getting the kids inside.

Specific places for the coats and the boots

Inside the mudroom, the marine theme continued with dark blue-green walls and high windows giving an underwater ambience to the place. Along one side of the room were pegs for hanging coats—half of them low on the wall for small kids and half of them higher for teenagers (drawing p. 35, left). Beneath the pegs, a bench provided a place to sit and put on shoes or take them off. Wet or muddy shoes were placed below the bench on wooden slats known as duckboards. Plastic trays slid into the 3-in. high space below the duckboards, where they caught shoe drippings. Shoes and boots tended to get stored on this duckboard surface for later use, so it also served as a shoe shelf for the whole family. Adjacent to this area were cubbies for mittens, hats, and scarves.

Mudrooms are for pets, too

On the opposite wall, below the adults' coats, were the dog beds (drawing p. 35, right) and, adjacent to them, the dog shower, which we also used to clean off exceptionally muddy boots before setting them on the duckboards to drip-dry. A dog shower—really just a basin set at floor level with a flexible hose and spray nozzle about 18 in. off the floor—may seem like an

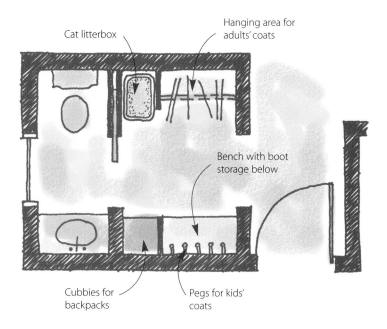

Cat litterbox

Hanging area for adults' coats

Bench with boot storage below

Cubbies for backpacks

Pegs for kids' coats

This scaled-down mudroom borrows heavily from its big brother.
No matter what its size, a good mudroom will have several elements in common. In this more modest version, many patterns remain the same: proximity to traffic flow; coat pegs at kid height; shoe storage; a drip area for wet footwear; a bench; cubbies for purses, backpacks, mittens, and hats; a hanging area for adults' coats; a pet area; and a half-bath nearby.

unnecessary extravagance. But in areas where rain and mud are a fact of life, it can make everyday living much more manageable. Muddy footprints can be restricted to the mudroom, with its easily cleanable tile floor. And the dogs were so accustomed to being cleaned up before they were allowed to enter the house proper that they would obediently crowd into the shower for the paw rubdown upon returning home, even when it was dry and clear outside. They seemed to enjoy the attention.

There was also a place next to the shower for dog-food storage, with food and water bowls just below, out of sight from the rest of the house but easily accessible for the dogs. Pet food bowls and other paraphernalia are frequently forgotten in home design. You walk into new homes across the country to find everything in its place, except for a huge dog cage in the middle of the kitchen floor. It's not that the new owners didn't know they

would need a place for Spot when they were out of the house, or when guests were over, but somehow the issue never came up with the architect or the builder. My friend's house, however, had a most attentive designer, and the dogs were put up in style.

Personal lockers for additional storage

These features would have been more than sufficient for most families, but this home was, after all, a country estate. So there was yet more storage for each family member. Along the back wall were four lockers, much like those you might find at the local gym today. These lockers, however, were made of wood, and when all were closed, they looked like a wall of cabinet doors. Inside each were more pegs for hanging personal items and a drawer below for treasures. My friend's drawer was full of pieces of old broken china she'd found on the family's property over the years.

Today in high-end mudrooms, lockers are a favored feature. Made either with or without doors, they allow family members to have their own storage place. They can be used in lieu of other hanging options if the mudroom is used exclusively by family. But if guests also use the area, be sure to include a few additional pegs.

The sports cupboard

Another feature I remember about my friend's mudroom was the sports cupboard—what in America we'd call a closet. The walls of this closet were lined with pegboard and covered with hooks supporting everything from tennis racquets to badminton net and shuttlecocks to croquet mallets. Although our American sports equipment differs somewhat in type, the concept is still a good one if you have space. A closet for outdoor-sports equipment such as skis, in-line skates, and skateboards makes eminently good sense to locate here. And if you can line the walls with hooks, you'll be able to get a lot more into it without having an avalanche each time you open the doors.

Although this baronial mudroom is obviously a spectacular—and in many ways extravagant—example, it contains within it all the features I hear being requested today. You can, of course, build a compact version that still meets the vast majority of your needs (drawing p. 37).

The Kitchen/ Family Room Relationship

Unless you live in an old house that hasn't been remodeled, it's easy to forget that kitchens used to be isolated workspaces, closed off from the rest of the house. This was largely because, before the invention of good extractor fans, food preparation was smelly. It just wasn't good taste to let these odors pervade the house. In addition, the mess generated from meal preparation was something to be kept hidden from the more formal civility of the living room.

Today, with the advent of the two-income family and the related reduction in shared family time, meal preparation has turned into family social hour as well. The kitchen is the common ground in the house. Everyone ends up there, and as a consequence, kitchens have expanded to provide more space for this socializing. The result is the kitchen/family room combination. What most people haven't considered, however, is

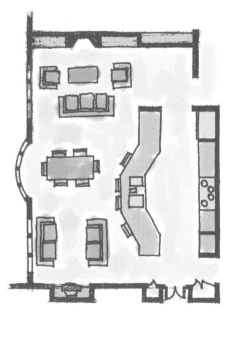

The undifferentiated great-room space. This plan, which gained popularity in the mid-1980s, offers little in the way of retreat from kitchen-related activity. When combined with a vaulted ceiling, the clatter of kitchen utensils becomes a serious annoyance.

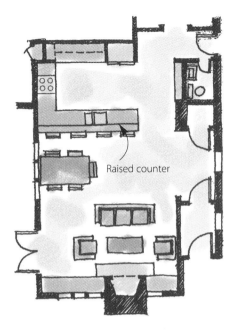

Raised counter

Screen the mess with a raised counter.
A 6-in.-high ledge above the standard-height kitchen counter obscures the kitchen from view. In a dead-end kitchen, such as this one, escaping from this spot during parties becomes a problem.

just how much the connection between these two rooms affects the livability of the home. For the majority of families and couples today, the isolated kitchen is a serious inconvenience. But kitchens that are completely open to the family room can also be a problem. The ideal for most households lies somewhere in between.

Managing the mess

A common concern about the kitchen is that if it is too much a part of the family room, the mess of pots, pans, plates, and potato peelings will color the experience of the entire family area. This is a frequent complaint that my clients have about homes with one large, undifferentiated great-room space, such as the one shown in the drawing on p. 39. Although it was a popular plan in the 1980s, people quickly discovered some inherent shortcomings to the big, dramatic space. Even though this organization does not physically impede family socializing, acoustically and visually, it takes over. Especially when such a room is built with a tall ceiling, as many were, just the normal clatter of dishes and pans can reverberate through the space, causing low-level irritation and making such activities as TV watching difficult.

So when I am designing a new home or remodeling an existing one, I try to give the kitchen some "psychological" distance from the family room, without separating the two. In this way, whoever is engaged in meal preparation can still participate in family interaction while keeping the acoustical and visual disruptions to a minimum. The following generic solutions work well to accomplish this separation:

1. **A raised counter acts as a screen.** Raising the height of the counter separating kitchen from family room creates a bar for guests and family to sit at while food is being prepared (drawing above). Once the meal is served and everyone is seated at the table, the raised counter obscures the view of dirty dishes and meal-prep

mess from the diners' view. For cooks who are embarrassed about the disorder left in their wake, this solution works well. Its drawbacks are that for families with small children, the countertop seating (bar stools) is generally too high for small children to hoist themselves up comfortably. And the raised counter works best as a screening device when it's part of a peninsula, rather than an island. Be aware also that a peninsula kitchen can be a problem during parties, when everyone congregates in there leaving no escape route.

2. **A partitioned alcove hides everything.** Some homeowners recognize the ambivalence they feel toward the kitchen. They realize that despite their best efforts at keeping the kitchen sights and sounds away from their guests, the guests seem to gravitate to the more informal parts of the house, most particularly to the kitchen. There is something reassuring—and more real—about the kitchen than almost any other part of the house. Perhaps it is that we can be assured of finding some sort of activity here.

By locating the kitchen in an alcove that can be partitioned off with sliding panels, the informal parts of the house can also be used for entertaining without having the kitchen mess on display while we're eating and socializing after a meal (drawing below).

3. **Counters, islands, and upper cabinets used as partial screens.** When total screening of the kitchen from the dining area isn't an issue, I prefer to use an island or peninsula at the same height as the rest of the countertop to create psychological separation (drawing on p. 42). An island provides a center for the kitchen and something for noncooks to lean on or sit at while food is being pre-

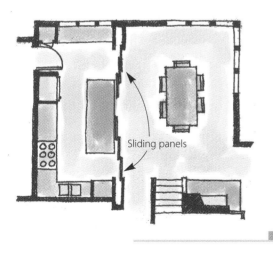

Sliding panels

The disappearing kitchen.
A kitchen in an alcove can be screened from view with sliding panels. The panels are concealed in wall pockets when not in use.

Upper cabinets

Island living with upper cabinets.
Standard-height counters, along with a row
of upper cabinets, give a sense of separation
between the kitchen and the dining area. The
bottom of the upper cabinets should be even
with the eye level of the tallest occupant.

*With the advent of the two-income family and
the related reduction in shared family time,
meal preparation has turned into family
social hour as well. The kitchen is the
common ground in the house.*

pared, without getting in the way. With
the counter surface at the regular 3-ft.
height, bar stools are at a child-friendly
height. It is also easier at this height to
have others help out with chopping, stir-
ring, or tasting. A taller counter section
makes it a lot more difficult for volunteer
cooks to help with the cooking. Try carv-
ing a Thanksgiving turkey on a 42-in.-
high surface, and you'll see what I mean.

Upper cabinets can also accentuate a
sense of separation without obstructing
the view. The height of the bottom of the
upper cabinet, however, is important to
making this work (drawing left). I usually
take the eye height of the tallest person in
the house and make that the height of the
upper-cabinet base.

Most people are familiar with houses
from the 1950s and 1960s, where upper
cabinets were brought down to within
15 in. of the peninsula or island countertop. There are few things more irritating
than having to bend over every time you
want to talk to someone on the other side
of the counter.

4. **An informal nook can be a buffer zone.**
Another way to create more psychological
separation between the kitchen and the
family room, without closing them off, is
to place an informal eating area between
the two (drawing facing page). Someone
working in the kitchen is not isolated, but
kitchen and family room are more clearly
separate rooms.

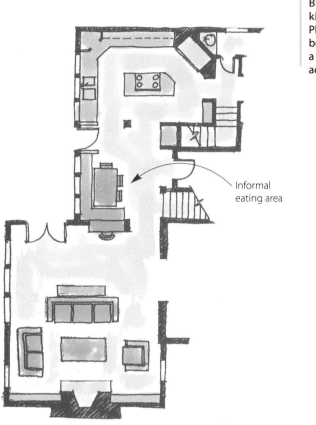

Buffer zone between the kitchen and the family room. Placing an informal eating area between the two rooms creates a lively spot that shares in the activity of both spaces.

Informal eating area

This is one of my favorite solutions, and it seems to satisfy the concerns of many couples regarding the level of connection between the two. From the family room, it feels as though the kitchen were more tucked away, while from the kitchen you can participate in the conversation taking place in the family room. With this arrangement, the eating area also tends to get heavily used, both for eating and for socializing, precisely because it is close to the kitchen.

So when you are planning to remodel or build new, start by thinking about the connection you desire between the kitchen and family room. Your answer, as you can see, will dramatically affect how the house works for everyday living.

Designing a Family Room That Works

For most households, the family room presents a significant design challenge because it is expected to do so much. It is really the living room of our era. But because "living room" usually connotes a formal living room, we've had to find another name. The family room is typically close to the kitchen, where the family can hang out together. Activities to be accommodated can vary widely, depending on the family in question, as can the relative degree of formality or informality.

In the time I've been working as a residential architect—almost two decades at this point—the functions of the room have changed socially, too, as technology has marched fearlessly into the twenty-first century. Today's family room, for example, often includes a computer station. This was unheard of not too long ago.

Accommodating multiple activities

When designed well, a family room can become the social hub of the house, providing space for any of the following activities and functions:

- TV watching
- Listening to music
- Congregating around a fire
- Enjoying the view outside
- Letting sunshine in
- Curling up with a good book
- Reading the paper
- Doing homework

When designed well, a family room can become the social hub of the house.

- Paying bills
- Engaging in hobbies
- Children's playing
- Adults' games
- Entertaining
- Socializing
- Eating and drinking
- Playing computer games
- Surfing the Internet and Web
- Snoozing

Just looking at the list, you can see the fundamental difficulty of successfully designing such a room. There can be so much going on that trying to make it do all things well runs the risk of making the room either enormous or schizophrenic, or both. With a little planning, and the recognition that not all activities happen simultaneously, it is possible to accommodate all these things and still maintain a sense of harmony and comfort.

The three most commonly identified activity wishes for a typical family room are

TV watching, gathering around the fireplace, and looking out the windows at the view beyond. For most people, these activities produce a conundrum because all three require viewing and all want to be the center of attention in the room, seemingly precluding the presence of one another (drawing p. 46, top).

Prioritizing focal points

When we analyze how we view each, though, we discover that there is at least one solution, and usually more than one, that allows all three activities to coexist comfortably. You can see from the drawings above that they don't have to be in conflict with one another. The TV requires the most focused attention and thus needs to be most focal to the sitting circle. The fireplace should be within view of the main seating arrangement but does not really require the front-and-center location that has traditionally been the case when access to radiant heat

A visual hierarchy.
Television viewing is a focused activity, requiring the TV to be located at the center of the sitting circle. The fireplace is typically something we glance at occasionally as we are doing other things. It does not require center-stage placement to be appreciated. Similarly, the view to the outside can surround us and give us pleasure without being the center of attention.

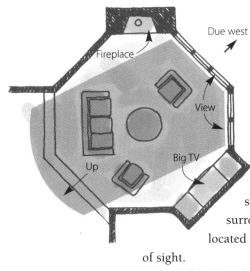

Good intentions gone bad.
This is probably the most poorly designed family room that I've come across (its 18-ft. ceiling, angled walls, and tall windows also made it expensive). The designer wanted to make the most of the view but made the room difficult to furnish. Worse yet, the westerly exposure created so much heat gain that the curtains had to be closed every afternoon.

was paramount. And the view to the great outdoors, even if it is stunningly beautiful, can surround us rather than be located in a singular direct line of sight.

Both the TV and the fireplace communicate with us through patterns of light that are less intense than daylight. So if you are attempting to view either one during the day, an adjacent window may cause squinting as you try to adjust your eyes to the less-bright image on which you are focusing attention. But sometimes there is just no other good alternative, and some compromise is in order.

For example, a TV flanked by windows (drawing A below) can be viewed during the day if the windows have shades. Another solution is to put the TV on a pull-out cart that can be turned toward the seating arrangement (drawing B below).

A place for everything

And what about all the other stuff on the list of activities that take place in a family room? One of my favorite approaches to their accommodation is to add a couple of alcoves that can each comfortably house several activities (drawings on facing page). For example, to the seating arrangement described earlier, you can add a desk

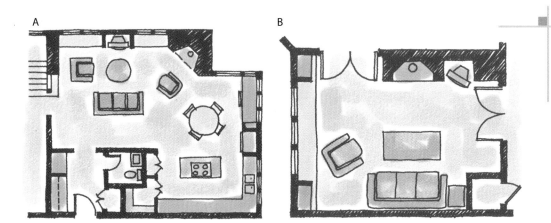

Two workable plans.
Windows on both sides of this TV (left) make it difficult to see the screen during the day, but in all other respects, this is a desirable configuration. When the TV is not located in the center of the sitting arrangement (right), placing it on an adjustable pull-out can improve viewing.

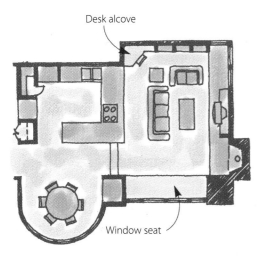

Desk alcove

Window seat

Desk alcove

Window seat

Alcoves expand a room's usefulness.
Adding a desk alcove and a window seat to these family-room layouts makes them into very versatile rooms. Notice the proximity of the informal eating areas.

alcove, where the computer and printer are located, where the children can do homework, and where adults can pay bills. The second alcove might be a wide window seat, where the children can play, where someone can curl up with a book, and where the newspaper can be spread out on Sunday morning.

In addition, if the informal eating area is close at hand and can be used for card playing, for hobbies, and for informal entertaining, the list of activities cited above can be accommodated in a room that is not much bigger than one containing only the main seating area. Each alcove defines its territory with walls and ceilings but doesn't need to be big to serve its several functions.

If you'd like to read more on alcoves, there is a wonderful section in *A Pattern Language* by Christopher Alexander et al (Oxford University Press, 1977) that describes the concept in far more detail than I can do here. Just because a room is intended

to house a lot of functions doesn't mean it needs to be large. In fact, such a room is often both more comfortable and more functional if it is kept to a reasonable minimum so that everyone using the room can feel part of the greater whole, rather than simply being a separate and isolated entity.

By analyzing each of the primary activities, determining what the needs of each are, and then combining the outcome of this analysis into a single solution, you are engaging in one of the fundamental processes of design. Often there are excellent solutions to problems that seem unsolvable at first glance.

So next time you find yourself thinking that you have two or three mutually exclusive focuses for your attention in a room, look deeper into each activity, and you may find a solution that weaves all of them together in a richer, more life-enhancing way than if you had tackled each of them separately, designing independent spaces for each.

Designing with Furnishings in Mind

When planning a new house or an addition to an existing one, we tend to focus first and foremost on floor-plan issues: which room is adjacent to which, what are their relative sizes, where do the windows go. Although the floor plan is important, its predominance is overrated. There are many other aspects of design that affect how well a house "lives," and high on that list is furniture, both type and arrangement. Surprisingly, though, we rarely give much thought to how a space will be furnished until the floor plan is decided on.

If you have existing furniture or know what new furniture you want to accommodate in your new home or addition, waiting too long to think about where it will go can be a mistake. You can actually start with the furniture, design the house to fit the best arrangements, and end up with a smaller, better-tailored house as a result.

Make an inventory of your furniture

Many architects will ask their clients what existing furniture they plan to bring to a new home or addition. Some people are embarrassed by the question. "Oh, don't worry about the furniture," they'll say. "We can think about that later." But by putting off this discussion, the architect must make the rooms large enough to accommodate the biggest couch, chairs, and dining table. So it can be helpful to take an inventory of what you possess and decide what you really want to keep, what can be disposed of, and what you might want in the future.

I suggest that my clients put together a photo album of all the furnishings in their current house before we start the design process. I ask them to measure each piece, being sure to include height as well as width and length, and to include rugs, paintings,

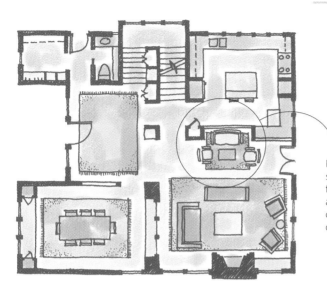

Oriental-rug collection dictates room sizes. Knowing the size of each rug from the beginning of the design process, the architect scaled each room to fit the rug specified for that room.

Pretty but uncomfortable, a setting of antique East Lake furniture sits in its own alcove where the owners can enjoy looking at it without it being in the way.

and other special treasures that will need a place. They also indicate on each image where in the new house or addition they see the item being located.

An excerpt from your list might look something like this:

Dining Table
42" wide x 78" long x 30" high
Extends to 96" long
To be located in dining area off kitchen

Couch
28" wide x 80" long x 31" high
To be located either in new living area or downstairs TV room. May decide to get new couch, depending on character of room.

Coffee Table
42" square x 15" high
Currently in family room. Depending on shape of room, could go in living area or TV room.

Side tables (2)
20" square
We'll likely dispose of these or possibly use them in guest bedroom. They have sentimental value since we bought them on our honeymoon; but they're pretty beat up and not suitable for the living room.

Oriental Rug
72" wide x 96" long

Definitely needs to go in the main living area. We love this rug, and the colors will probably influence our selection of carpet and tile in this area.

Painting of Old Barn
45" wide x 29" high
To be hung above the fireplace in the living area if possible, though we'd be open to other ideas.

Although this exercise may seem like overkill, when a house or addition is being custom designed, such specificity can really help the architect make the house a personal

It often surprises people to find out how many objects of significance they actually own. They may not be of high monetary value, but they have a lot of meaning to family members and thus are worthy of a special spot in the home.

expression of the inhabitants' lives. For example, if I know that my client has a number of Oriental rugs and if I have the sizes of those rugs as I start designing, I can proportion each room to accommodate rug and associated furniture arrangements (drawing p. 49). Or if I know the dimensions of an antique dresser, I can design a special niche to feature it. Without this information, such a piece would simply end up being pushed against the wall somewhere. It often surprises people to find out how many objects of significance they actually own. They may not be of high monetary value, but they have a lot of meaning to family members and thus are worthy of a special spot in the home.

What should you do with heirloom furniture that doesn't suit your lifestyle?

Another somewhat touchy issue has to do with family history: namely, what to do with furniture that has been handed down to you but doesn't really work for your lifestyle. Many of us tend to decorate our homes for looks and nostalgia rather than for comfort. Both are important, but if a space is to be used today, it definitely needs to be comfortable, or it will sit idle.

As our lifestyles have become more informal, much of the formal furniture of past centuries has lost its appeal. We don't often

Designing around the owners' furniture can yield a smaller house.
This floor plan was designed around the owners' collection of Scandinavian furniture. If the sizes of the furniture had not been known, the living room, for instance, would have had to be bigger to accommodate the larger American furniture that's more typical today.

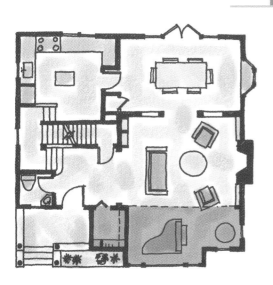

A piano alcove improves the house. A small addition (shaded area) not only made room for a new grand piano but also enlarged the living room and improved the character of the front of the house.

sit in straight-back chairs, sipping tea out of bone-china teacups with formal guests any more. So late Aunt Ginny's beautiful living-room furniture sits in wait, filling the largest room in the house in readiness for an event that doesn't happen in our present-day world.

When designing new space, you have to decide how much you are going to dedicate to such heirloom pieces. If money is tight, I will often suggest that my clients consider one of the following options:

- Place the heirloom pieces in locations where they can be seen and appreciated, but where they don't take up primary living space.
- Design a special alcove for one or two of the pieces so that they can be seen but not used, and then put the rest in storage.
- Place all of them in storage until you win the lottery.
- Give the furniture to another family member who has room to house the pieces.

Although these suggestions may seem heartless, many people sacrifice their own comfort to provide display space for family history. For those with the budget to do so, there's no reason not to, but with new space costing what it does, devoting large areas to furniture arrangements that will never be used is an extravagance that may not be sensible. If that money is used instead to make the primary living spaces more comfortable and hospitable, it can have a much greater impact on the home's livability.

Let's look at some examples

Several years ago, one couple asked me to design a new house to accommodate their wonderful collection of Scandinavian furniture. Scandinavian furniture tends to be smaller than its American counterpart, so I was able to tailor the spaces to fit the furniture perfectly (drawing facing page). Another couple was planning to remodel their existing home to accommodate a grand piano. They had planned to add 10 ft. to the entire front of the house, but we pointed out that by adding a much smaller area, an alcove specifically for the piano, they could save money, make the living room more in scale with the rest of the house, and improve the character of the front of the house at the same time (drawing above).

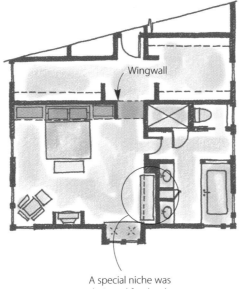

Wingwall

A special niche was designed for the dresser, giving it a built-in look.

Room for tansu nightstands. Nestled beneath a lowered ceiling (shaded area) and protected by a wingwall, this king-size bed is flanked by Japanese tansus.

Because a grand piano has a highly refined shape and looks best when seen from the side, the alcove was designed to accentuate this face, making it visible from both living room and dining room.

When designing bedrooms, especially those with tall ceilings, I like to lower the area over the head of the bed to give a sense of shelter. If I know the size of the bed and the side tables, I'll often add wingwalls to the sides to increase that shelter and to protect the sleepers from direct view of the door to the room. In this example (drawing left), the clients wanted to put wider-than-standard Japanese tansus on the sides of their king-size bed, so I knew from the beginning of the design process that the bedroom had to have a wall long enough to house these items.

Contrary to what you might believe, such specifics actually help make a design interesting. The more I know about my clients' likes, dislikes, collections, furniture, and special objects, the easier it is to make their houses both delightful to live in and beautiful to look at. It's as though each item acts as a catalyst for creativity, and what results is a richness of detail and composition in which everything seems to fit just right. Our furniture helps define our living patterns, and by knowing what sizes, shapes, and arrangements are preferred, the design can truly be tailored to how we live.

Putting the TV in Its Place(s)

Many technological advances have affected our living patterns at home over the past few decades, but none has had such a dramatic impact as television. Residential architects are very much aware of the differences in TV-watching habits from family to family. Some people want TVs in every room, while others have all but banished TV from the house. These patterns are seldom discussed, but they are of enormous importance in a home.

It is common for husbands and wives to disagree on where TVs should go and how much TV they want to watch.

Survey family viewing habits

Whether you are simply rearranging the furniture in your existing home, adding on, or building a new house, you first need to analyze your TV-viewing habits. Where are the televisions now? Who watches them and at what locations? What are the positives and negatives of each location? A project I did recently for a couple with twin 6-year-old boys can help to illustrate this process.

In their current house (drawing p. 54), Kate and Ray had these TVs:

Kitchen TV: A 13-in. model on the countertop in the corner. Watched by Kate while cooking dinner.

Positives: Easy to see from everywhere in the kitchen.

Negatives: Takes up precious counter space. Not connected to cable, so picture not good and limited channel choices.

Family-room TV: A 27-in. model on a TV cart in the corner of the room. Watched by the kids most frequently during the day. Watched by Ray and the kids in evening (Kate doesn't really like to watch

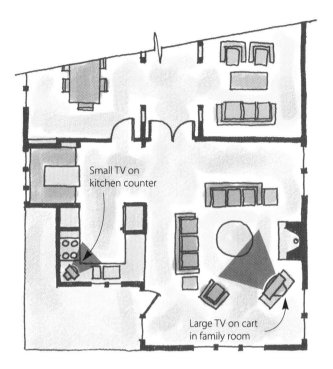

Small TV on
kitchen counter

Large TV on cart
in family room

Dueling televisions.
In the original arrangement
of the house, one television
sat on a cart in the corner of
the family room and the
other on the kitchen counter.
This placement resulted in
constant TV noise throughout this part of the house
and disagreements over
which programs to watch.

a lot of TV, so she tends not to watch it
unless it's a movie).

Positives: Easy to see from everywhere in
the family room.

Negatives: Makes it difficult to do anything else in this room while the TV is on.
Often causes arguments during meal prep
when Kate wants to watch the news in the
kitchen, and children want to watch their
programs in the family room.

Master-bedroom TV: A 19-in. model on
dresser across from bed. Watched by Ray
before going to sleep at night. Kids watch
cartoons in the morning.

Positives: Good location to be seen
from bed.

Negatives: Kate doesn't like TV in bedroom. She prefers to read before going to
sleep but can't do so with TV on. Kids
pile into master bedroom each morning
to watch cartoons from the bed. On week-
days, this routine really slows down the
getting-up process.

Often, until you've made such a list, you
are unaware of one another's likes and dislikes and don't realize how much the location of a particular TV affects your living
patterns. For example, until Kate and Ray did
the survey, Ray hadn't realized how much the
master-bedroom TV bothered Kate. When
couples start to work with an architect, this
sort of information often comes as a revela-
tion. Until such a habit is brought into aware-
ness and discussed, people will live with the
most inconvenient or irritating conditions,
never considering the option of moving the
offending TV to remedy the situation.

Put the survey results to work

The next step, then, is to consider how
you would like to live with the television. It is common for husbands and wives
to disagree on where TVs should go and
how much TV they want to watch. I recommend that each adult in the house make a
list. If there are children in the house, each
parent should also make note of how they

Pocket doors allow screen to be concealed when not in use.

Freeing some counter space.
Putting the TV in a cabinet above the wall ovens got it out of the way, and into a spot where it can be easily seen from the counters or from the new chair. The TV is mounted on a swivel base, allowing it to be turned toward either area.

New chair

envisage children's viewing habits. Using Kate and Ray as examples again, their lists were as follows:

Kate: "I'd like to keep a small TV in the kitchen, maybe also visible from the kitchen table, so that I can watch the news while I'm making meals. If we have a TV in the family room, I'd like it to be in a cabinet with doors so that it's not always staring at us when it's not on. I suspect the kids would be less insistent on turning it on if it weren't always within view.

"I wish there were a place I could go to be away from the TV sometimes because it seems it's always on when we're in the house. It really makes it difficult to do anything else and limits conversation. The kids watch too much TV in my opinion, but I don't know what to do to limit their viewing without being seen as unreasonable."

Ray: "I like to watch TV in the evenings. It's a way of calming down after the workday.

One of the problems is that the kids want to watch different programs than I do, so there's sometimes a battle. I don't really need to watch TV in bed. It's just a habit I've fallen into, I guess. Knowing how much it bothers Kate, I'd be comfortable with skipping it. The kids watch a lot of TV. I don't really mind this but wish there were a place where they could watch the programs they like without my having to hear the TV all the time."

Most of us are unaware of how greatly the location of a TV can affect both our lifestyles and our emotional well-being.

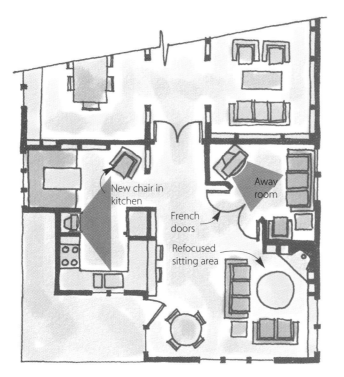

New chair in kitchen

French doors

Refocused sitting area

Away room

The remodeled solution. By creating a separate "away" room for the larger TV, sounds can be isolated, allowing other activities to occur in the main family area. The refocused sitting area in the family room is now available for reading, conversation, or projects at one of the two tables.

After couples have made their lists, there needs to be some discussion about how to accomplish the stated goals. The solution that we came up with for Kate and Ray was to provide two different TV areas: one for adult TV watching and one primarily for the kids' TV watching. We located a 19-in. TV above the double ovens in the kitchen, which Kate could see as she made dinner (drawing left). By adding a comfortable chair adjacent to the kitchen work area—what is commonly referred to as a hearth room these days—Ray could watch the same TV because both of them like to watch the news at that time of day. An added benefit is that they also use this time to compare notes on the day. Because they are in closer proximity now, they've found that they communicate more, which both of them really like.

Then we put the TV that had been in the family room into a new room, which we carved out of the existing family room (drawing above). This room, which I call the away room, has glass French doors that allow visual connection both to family room and kitchen but that offer acoustical separation. The kids can still see Mom and Dad while they watch TV, and they no longer argue with Dad about what program to watch.

But best of all, according to Kate, the family room is now used for a variety of other activities. There's more family interaction possible with the TV no longer the dominant force in the room. The corner where the TV used to be has become a projects space, with a small table for playing games, drawing, or making models. Ray can watch TV when he wants to in the away room, but interestingly, both he and the boys aren't watching as much, simply because there are now other things to do in the most social space in the house.

Kate and Ray's experience is not unusual. Most of us are unaware how greatly the location of a TV can affect both our lifestyles and our emotional well-being. However ridiculous it may seem, the tensions brought about by arguments over what TV program to watch can color the mood of an evening. If a simple analysis such as the example above can identify the root problem—in this case that children and adults wanted to watch different things—there can be a newfound peace in the house.

The more thoughtfully we consider the integration of television into our lives, the less likely it is that it will become a source of irritation. It can be such a powerful tool, both for education and for entertainment, but it can also become a home wrecker and a blight on family interaction if not thought about. So start with you current TV watching patterns, identify how you'd like to live with television, and then work together to find solutions that meet everyone's desires. You may need to make a few compromises along the way, but almost always, simply talking about it can bring forth solutions to visual and acoustical problems related to TV that you've been living with for years without even knowing it.

THREE

New Places for Not So New Things

A famous architect of the twentieth century, Le Corbusier, once dubbed the house "a machine for living." Although this phrase caused him no end of controversy during his life time and has been the topic of much architectural debate in the decades since his death, there's an aspect of the phrase that is right on. Our houses have all sorts of functions to perform, and just like a well-oiled machine, a well-designed house can take care of these functions almost effortlessly. By contrast, one that is based only on design solutions from the past is apt to present difficulties that make the "machine for living" belch and stutter. The functions that it now accommodates are very different from those of the past, though they may carry the same name.

The most obvious example is the pantry. If you base the design of a pantry on what was needed 50 years ago you won't have nearly enough storage space. Storage needs are very different today, with warehouse quantities of toilet paper, and huge flats of soda. Although we use the same word, *pantry*, to describe the food storage area in the house, its basic characteristics need to be reevaluated.

This is true for a number of the functions we now put our houses to, whether it be recycling or conducting business from home. Although we think we know what needs we have, when you really stop and think about any of these functions, realize that your current house is very poorly designed to accommodate them.

My favorite example is the lack of a specific place for sorting the mail. Because it's a relatively new function, we haven't designated a place for it, and so all the mail lands on the most available surface— usually the dining room table or kitchen island. Many of this country's dining rooms should really be renamed the "mailing sorting place" since this has become their primary purpose in life.

So what you'll be learning in this section is how to look at the specific functions we engage in within our homes, how to analyze our needs with respect to them, and how to rethink their designs so that they really work for the way we live today. In so doing, just like a well-oiled machine, our houses can start to work better and help make life within them a graceful dance, rather than a constant battle.

A Porch for All Seasons

If you've ever owned a house with a real screen porch, with screening stretching from floor to ceiling and covering at least two full walls, you'll know what a wonderful addition to the living space it can provide. Although the porch is attached to the house, nothing about it feels interior. Instead, it's an outdoor room connected to nature but protected from such undesirable conditions as rain, bugs, and direct sunlight. In climates that are benign year-round, the screen porch can be a perfect solution for outdoor living, but in most areas, there are extended periods when the screen porch sits dormant, waiting for summer.

Architects and designers are often presented with a dilemma when their clients wish for both a screen porch and a sunroom: the screen porch for the warmer months, the sunroom for cooler ones. Because most clients' budgets won't allow for both spaces, the screen porch is deleted from the wish list in deference to a room that can be used year-round. The sad result, however, is that the homeowners never have the experience of being outside when they're at home. A sunroom, even one with many openable windows, still feels like the indoors.

Over the years, I've kept my eyes open for clever ideas that allow a porch to serve both functions. My examples illustrate four solutions that can offer both indoor and outdoor living, depending on the season. With a little bit of effort, you can have the best of both worlds without the extra cost of building two rooms for the same basic purpose.

The screen porch with glass panels

This solution is the least expensive, offering year-round living in all but the coldest climates. In the summer, this is simply a standard screen porch. But come cooler months, glass or acrylic panels are clipped into the screened openings to enclose the space from the elements (drawing facing page). Typically, single-pane glass is used, so the room will be expensive to heat. But for a room that's used only once in a while during the winter, it's ideal.

In most places, you can find local fabricators for glass or acrylic panels—from hardware stores to glass suppliers to your own general contractor. Some use an aluminum edge strip with butterfly clips at two or three locations along each edge, while others capture the inside edge of the panel with removable wooden stops.

It's also worth noting that because these panels are typically made to order, this solution is an easy retrofit. Even if your screen porch was not originally intended for use as a year-round porch, it can be converted inexpensively into one that works adequately, as long as heating is not required. There is also the added benefit that the room stays significantly cleaner without the buildup of winter snow, dust, and debris.

Heating for such a porch generally comes in one of two forms: electric baseboard, which is cheap to install but expensive to run, or in-floor heating, installed on a separate zone from the rest of the house. In warmer climates, you can also use a hotel-room-size heat pump, which is significantly more efficient than electric baseboard but noisier, as anyone who has recently tried to sleep in a hotel room can attest. It's best to check with your building officials about local regulations as well. Some cold-climate areas that have special energy-efficiency codes actually prohibit the heating of a glassed-in porch because of the amount of energy

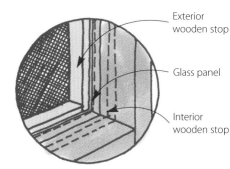

Exterior wooden stop

Glass panel

Interior wooden stop

Weatherizing a standard screen porch.
The classic screen porch can be enclosed with glass or acrylic panels fabricated locally and held in place by wooden stops.

required. If the system is clearly separate from the rest of the house, however, it is usually allowed, with the assumption that you will turn it on only when the room is in use.

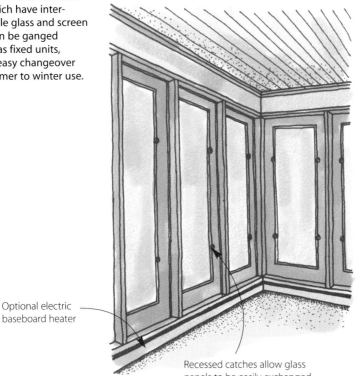

Combination doors allow easy conversion. Combination storm/screen doors, which have interchangeable glass and screen panels, can be ganged together as fixed units, allowing easy changeover from summer to winter use.

Optional electric baseboard heater

Recessed catches allow glass panels to be easily exchanged with screen panels.

The porch with combination doors

One of my favorite screen-porch/sunroom solutions, which I learned from a general contractor 20 years ago, is to use a series of wooden storm/screen combination doors as panels between 2×4 framing (drawing left). These doors are made to allow a glass panel to be interchanged with a screen panel according to the season. The doors, purchased before they've been drilled for door hardware, make a perfect wall system for a porch. In addition, by making one of the panels into a real opening door, you have a seamlessly integrated design.

The only downside of this system is that somewhat less wall surface is screened because of the dimension of the door frames. Still, it produces an elegant look, and homeowners can easily change the panels from season to season with a minimum of hassle. And because you are removing the screen panels during the winter, more light reaches the interior as a result.

Heating solutions for this system are much the same as for clip-in panels. If you are planning to use electric baseboard, however, be sure to install the doors at least 5 in. above floor height so that you've got space to run the baseboard below them.

The sunroom with removable double-hung windows

Another alternative that has become an option with the advent of easily removable sash (the parts of the window that move) is to build a sunroom with floor-to-ceiling double-hung windows. In warmer months, you can remove the sash entirely, leaving just the screens on the exterior; then reinstall them in the winter to create an enclosed room (drawing right). You can even have double glazing with this option, because manufacturers make these windows either single- or double-glazed.

The reinstallation process for this solution can be a little more time-consuming because it's important to clean the vinyl channels carefully on each side of the windows so that the sash will operate easily. In most places, warm weather arrives gradually, so over a period of months, this option also allows for an in-between weather state, when the sash can be reinstalled and the double hungs used as, well, windows. By opening all the window units you have 50% of the potential screened area, with the option of closing the windows easily when either cold weather or an invasion of pollen makes greater enclosure desirable.

Although you might question the sense of removing window sashes in this manner, the difference in experience between a room

The double-hung window approach.
A porch enclosed with tall double-hung windows with removable sash allows the room to become a screen porch in the summer. The arrangement has the added advantage of operable windows for spring and fall, depending on the weather.

Double-hung window frames with sash removed

Even if your screen porch was not originally intended for use as a year-round porch, it can be converted inexpensively into one that works adequately as long as heating is not required.

A commercial option. Mon-Ray makes a porch enclosure called Glasswalls that consists of four stackable windows that can be retracted to allow up to 75% of the screened area to be exposed. Although not as authentic as true screen-porch panels, they come close, and the panels can be closed completely at a moment's notice in inclement weather.

surrounded by windows and one enclosed by screens alone is immense. For screen porch lovers, there's no comparison, and the wish to experience the great outdoors fully far outweighs the downsides of dust and exposure to the elements. This solution offers the best of all possible worlds for the porch lover: a room that can be turned into a normal sunroom for the months when a screen porch is unusable but that converts readily to an outdoor room when the weather allows.

A manufactured porch-window system

There are a number of companies around the country that manufacture porch-window systems that are intended to allow maximum flexibility for screen-porch/sunroom variety. Although these systems are a popular choice with consumers, the downside with most of the systems is that they are composed of sliding windows that give you only 50% open area, which still leaves you with the impression of an interior room, albeit a breezy one.

My favorite off-the-shelf porch-window system is made by Mon-Ray (800-544-3646) and allows several panes of glass to stack at the top of each window opening so that you have more than 75% of the glass area openable (drawing left). This result still feels more interior than a true screen porch, but it's the best option I've found for situations where you want to be able to close the windows in a downpour or on a chilly night.

To figure out which of the options works best for you, take a look at the times of year that you like to be in an indoor/outdoor setting. Recognize that the more openness you can have, the more "outdoors" the room will feel. And then weigh the relative costs and benefits of each of these systems. All of them are less expensive, obviously, than building two separate rooms for winter and summer use, but each is more expensive than a screen porch alone would be. Making the right choice for your own lifestyle can make a huge difference to the livability of the house all year long and for all the seasons you live there.

Designing a Mail-Sorting Place

There are many new devices to help our lives run more smoothly, and we adopt them with few complaints these days. We're getting used to the ever-increasing rate of change. We may be irritated that a piece of equipment we bought only a year or two ago is now radically out of date, but we seem to take it in stride. Product designers keep designing, and we keep consuming. Strange, then, that so many of the changes that have occurred in the way we use our homes haven't received equal atten-tion and haven't been attended to with the same entrepreneurial verve.

If we look carefully at how we really live in our houses, we can see where the short-comings of our current house designs lie. One of my favorite observations of a need waiting for a solution is the way many formal dining rooms are used today. I can't tell you how many homes I've been to where the dining-room table is covered with piles of mail. There's always an apology from the residents for their untidiness, but that's not what I'm seeing at all. Rather, I'm observing a new function with no place to go: a mail-sorting place.

The average household receives far more mail today than was typical even a decade ago, but we haven't accommodated this onslaught with a designated area in the house.

Individual mail slots

Catalogs to be recycled

Trash bin for junk mail

Sorting mail on the back-side of an island.
Many people bring mail directly into the kitchen where it covers the island, interfering with food preparation. Creating a mail-sorting area on the back side of the island can alleviate the problem.

The average household receives far more mail today than was typical even a decade ago, but we haven't accommodated this onslaught with a designated area in the house. So a room used only rarely for its official purpose becomes an ideal spot for this unnamed, and so unacknowledged, present-day need. If you're happy with housing this function in your dining room, there's no reason why you can't continue to do so. But for many households, there are better solutions if you simply spend a little time and effort considering the problem.

The following process is intended to help you determine both the best place to locate your own mail-sorting place and the best way to configure its layout for your household's patterns of behavior.

Where does the mail enter the house?

The first step in finding a solution is to look at how you handle the mail now. If yours is anything like most households, you pick up the mail from the mailbox on your way home from work, and you carry it into the house through the back door, along with your briefcase, purse, and other paraphernalia. Because few houses have a designated spot to put down the mail, it is usually treated unceremoniously. Many kitchen islands and peninsulas become the repository for unsorted mail, which can be a major inconvenience for the cook in the family. Kitchen-counter space is typically in short supply, so covering one of these primary work surfaces with papers doesn't endear the depositor to his or her mate. (We can make light of this, but it is such seemingly insignificant behavior patterns that can drive couples to distraction.)

As I mentioned, the dining-room table is another favorite mail-deposit site. It's out of the way of major work surfaces, but piles of mail on the dining table are not always appreciated for their aesthetic contribution. Some people choose to put all incoming mail into a large basket after reviewing it briefly for important envelopes requiring immediate attention. Others take the mail directly to the home office, even when it is inconveniently distant from the point of entry.

As you can see quickly, there's clearly a problem here. All the different types of mail are bundled together, from junk mail to catalogs to magazines to bills to personal correspondence. Each type of mail requires a very different type of attention—and much of it is best disposed of almost immediately.

Identifying possible locations for the new mail-sorting place

One thing I've discovered as an architect is that no matter how brilliant the design, if it isn't a natural outgrowth of

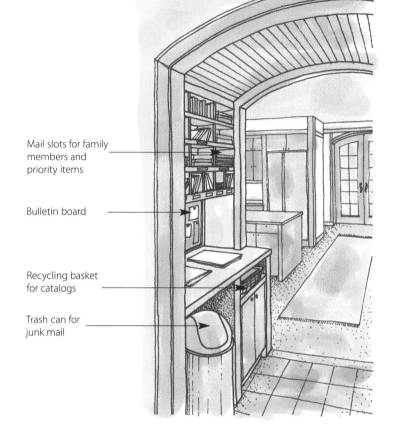

Mail slots for family members and priority items

Bulletin board

Recycling basket for catalogs

Trash can for junk mail

On the edge of the action. A mail-sorting place works best for most households when it has a good view into the main living area but isn't right in the middle of everything.

existing habits, it rarely works. For example, if one member of a couple is untidy by nature and untroubled by a countertop covered with mail, a new design isn't going to make that person any tidier. So the design solution needs to take into account the inevitable untidiness, perhaps by placing it behind doors, where it's easily accessible from the point of entry but out of sight when doors are closed.

The following is a list of the most frequently identified location options. But don't let these choices constrain you. If you think another option is more appropriate for your family, go with your intuition.

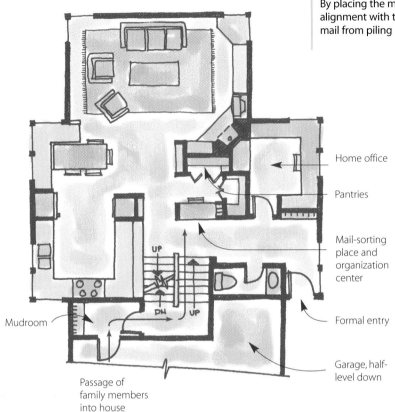

Keeping mail out of the kitchen, but close to a main walkway. By placing the mail-sorting area next to the kitchen and in direct alignment with the family's path into the house, you can prevent mail from piling up on the kitchen counter.

Home office

Pantries

Mail-sorting place and organization center

Formal entry

Garage, half-level down

Mudroom

Passage of family members into house

The kitchen island or peninsula

Most families bring mail to the most convenient "spreading out" room, with is usually the kitchen. And if there's a wide area of countertop at its center—such as an island or peninsula—then this will be the favorite spot for mail sorting. But if it is to work as a mail-sorting place rather than just a dumping ground, there must be places to put the sorted mail readily at hand (drawing p. 66). An island can be designed with a segment of lowered counter with mail slots nearby for separating mail according to recipient or priority. If the island is wide enough, the slots can be provided right there. If not, then allow the island surface to function as the sorting area and provide the mail-slot area a few steps away so that it's easy to follow through on the sorting. Without this convenience, the system won't work.

Make sure there's a place for a good-size trash can or paper-recycling bin. And if you are able to recycle catalogs in your area, put those that you don't want directly into a re-cycling basket built in to the mail-sorting place. For those catalogs you want to keep around, I'd suggest a basket or magazine holder that will allow you to look through them at your leisure. I've seen people locate the "to look at later" basket in a variety of places, from the family room to the bath-room to the informal eating area. Just make sure you develop a routine for purging that basket every week or two.

The kitchen desk

If you can get family members to comply, another system is to locate a desk space in a convenient spot adjacent to the kitchen where it can serve both as a mail-sorting place and as an organization center (drawing p. 67). You can keep a calendar here, plenty of bulletin-board space, a place to recharge cell phones, and even a computer with Internet hookup. By locating this hub slightly away from the center of the kitchen, you don't run the risk of having papers all over the island. But it's important to recognize that human nature is to lay claim to the most convenient space. So if the kitchen desk is to function properly for mail sorting, it has to be easier to use than the island. If it's closer to the point of entry, it'll usually work. And as with the kitchen-island solution, don't forget to build in facilities to deal with the junk mail and recyclables.

The everyday entry

If you have a house with a spacious everyday entry, the path into the house from the garage, for example, consider it for the mail-sorting function. You can do the separating of junk mail before it comes any farther into the house, and the trash bin is easily emptied into the outside garbage cans on a regular basis.

What is not obvious about this solution, however, is that in practice, many people still bring mail into the main living area of the house because they want to feel as though they've arrived home before starting to do anything else.

If you select this solution, make sure that you are close enough to main living areas to reinforce the feeling of being home. The best way to do this is to establish a good visual connection between the mail-sorting place and the kitchen. The function itself doesn't need to be visible from the kitchen, but someone standing at the mail-sorting counter should be able to see directly into the kitchen.

Designing the place itself

Here's a list of the most common elements of a well-designed mail-sorting place. These elements will vary depending on your needs, but this checklist is a good start.

- Pigeon slots for individual mail. Make sure they are sized appropriately for the quantities received by each individual.
- A separate slot for bills or other important mail requiring immediate attention. Some households may require one of these for each adult if different individuals take care of different functions, or if one or more individuals work from home.
- A place for catalogs you want to keep. To be transferred ASAP to the "to look at later" basket.
- A recycling bin for catalogs you don't want to keep.
- A recycling bin and/or trash can for wastepaper and junk mail. Make sure that it's big enough for you to throw out immediately the stuff you don't want.
- An optional bulletin board or message board.

Home-Office Design: Where to Put One

When people build or remodel today, they often need to include a space that was a rarity until recently: a home office. The advent of the computer has allowed work to be done quickly and effectively from home, and more people are doing just that. For many, home is a far more conducive environment for concentration.

When I had an architecture practice in the Twin Cities and I really needed to focus, I went home to an environment where I was in control of the phone and where there were no interruptions from colleagues or clients. For families, however, if the home office isn't hidden away, interruptions can become a serious impediment to productivity. For some, it's children; for others, it's the proximity of the refrigerator that causes scattered thinking.

We're all different, and circumstances vary. So there's no single solution to home-office location that works for everyone. To arrive at the best location and design for your situation, here are some guidelines to help you identify primary distraction potentials and the most conducive environments for clarity of thought.

If you have small children...

Something I've noticed about people who haven't spent much time working at home is their idealized impression of children's behavior. Over the years, I've had several clients who initially looked forward to working at home precisely because they could be close to their children every day. So they locate their home office on the main level, with doors separating that room from

If the home office isn't hidden away, interruptions can become a serious impediment to productivity.

main living spaces, assuming that this plan will ensure privacy when they need to work quietly.

But it doesn't usually work that way—especially with small children who don't normally see their parents much during the day. Even if the door is firmly shut, kids know (true or not) that Dad or Mom would really rather be playing with them, and they use every trick to lure them out. These interruptions can cause a lot of tension and frustration, so my usual recommendation is to put more separation between your work space and the primary social rooms.

The exception to this advice is if you are the primary caregiver for children while you work—not an ideal situation for kids or work. In this case, a main-level arrangement (drawing above), with visual access to kids' play areas, is a good solution. Keep in mind, though, that situations change. As children grow older, they typically need less supervision. The space you build for today's circumstances will also need to work 5 and 10 years from now. In your mind's eye, project forward and envision where children will likely be playing, doing homework, or watching TV, and make sure that these activities won't conflict with your office location. If you think they might, then look for another solution.

If you want to be alone...

For many people, a quiet environment with no distractions is the best place to work. So a good strategy is to start by identifying the most out-of-the-way places in the house, or the ones that are least used during the hours you normally work. A common solution is to add a small room that opens off the master bedroom, several doors away from the distractions of family activities (drawing p. 72). For other people, a converted attic at the top of the house or a bedroom at the end of a hallway can provide the necessary privacy.

If sound is a particular disruption and other members of the household are often using the TV or stereo, make sure that the space you choose is not directly above or below the source of the noise. Even if there's physical isolation, sound travels through

An office close to the heart of the house.
Locating an office adjacent to primary living space can be a good vantage point for supervising children but not good when there's work to do. Even with the door closed, children know you're within easy reach and will likely interrupt often.

floorboards and walls unless special measures have been taken during construction.

If your clients come to the house...

When you have a consulting practice in your home, the design challenge is increased substantially. If you are like most people, you won't want your clients to enter through the main living space in the house. By adding a separate entry or by creating a way to partition the front entry from views to the rest of the house, you can keep family spaces private and still give your clients a gracious welcome. There may be

need for a waiting area and certainly a powder room adjacent to your consultation room (drawing facing page). And for both family members and for clients, it's important to make the room acoustically private, either with added insulation at walls abutting living spaces or with in-between spaces, such as a butler's pantry or a closet.

My favorite solution for a client-friendly atmosphere is to make a separate entrance and to create a greater differentiation between living space and workspace. If you live in a climate where a lower level or basement is common, a walk-out lot with lower-level entrance can be ideal. You can accom-

The office as retreat within the house.
An office off a master-bedroom suite gives more privacy, especially when there are young children. If both the door to the bedroom and the door to the office are closed, it's a clear indication that Mommy or Daddy is busy. Because it's also far away from the living area, there's also less temptation to interrupt.

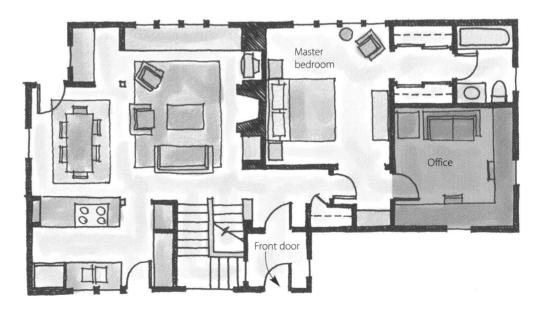

Master bedroom

Office

Front door

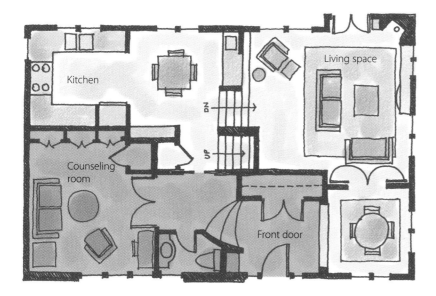

plish the same thing with an upper level, perhaps including an entrance at the midlevel stair landing. Or you can convert an existing garage into a home office.

If the refrigerator is hard to ignore...

If you are serious about working at home but find it difficult to separate yourself from the amenities of the household, another common option is to build a room above or adjacent to the garage. If it is a structure separate from the house, this solution offers several advantages. Even though the commute is short, you can increase the sense of "going to work." You are in a different environment, and it takes a more conscious and physical effort to make a trip back to the house.

The only major drawbacks are that most garages are uninsulated and have no plumbing, so in cold or hot climates, if you're remodeling, it's more difficult to create a comfortable environment. It can also be expensive if a new heating or cooling system is required. Because a garage is a separate structure, many local zoning codes will not allow a powder room to be installed to ensure that the space is not used as an apartment. So before proceeding with such a project, you should research the costs and constraints.

Don't forget ambiance

Wherever you locate the home office, don't forget that you'll be more likely to use it if it functions well and if it's a pleasant place to be. I've had clients tell me that their office can be anywhere in the house and doesn't require windows or views. But when I visit years later, I see that the spaces that weren't designed with light and comfort in mind have been abandoned, while those that were thoughtfully designed for maximum ambiance and functionality are still heavily used.

Making a Place of Your Own

In my experience, once a couple starts living together, all the rooms in the house become shared property. While the two people may have different tastes, necessary decorating compromises are made. The resulting decor becomes either an amalgam of their sensibilities, or one person's tastes dominate and the other makes do.

On the other hand, it's common today for each child to have his or her own bedroom, with personalized decoration. For some reason, however, we haven't extended this luxury to adults, although the idea appeals to many. The concept of a place of one's own seems almost taboo, with the implication that if you need a space for yourself, then maybe there are marital problems.

As an architect, I've observed the opposite. When each adult has a small place within the house to make entirely his or her own, the marriage is often healthier. It's human nature that we need places to be together and places to be apart.

We can design our homes to allow this need to be realized in hospitable ways. Whether it's a place to engage in a hobby, to listen to music, or simply to be quiet and away from the hubbub of family life for a while, such a spot can offer the opportunity to nurture individual delights and passions. The following anecdotes illustrate the variety of places of one's own that are possible, with ideas to meet every budget.

A divided office conquers two needs

Several years ago, I was hired by a newly married couple. Their house had been owned by Richard for more than a decade, and Joyce was the newcomer to the resi-

The concept of a place of one's own seems almost taboo, with the implication that if you need a space for yourself, then maybe there are marital problems.

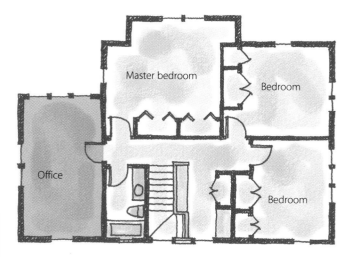

Dividing the office doubles its usefulness.
Before remodeling, the upstairs has three bedrooms and a fairly large office.

After remodeling, the office has been turned
into two smaller offices, giving both adults
places of their own.

dence. His tastes leaned toward darker finishes and color schemes with a distinctly
masculine flavor, while she preferred a light,
soft, contemporary look. They'd succeeded
in redoing the decor of the house more or
less to satisfy both of them, but it was not a
complete expression of either of their sensibilities. Joyce suggested that perhaps there
was a way they could also have a small place
where each could decorate the way they
wanted. Richard could put up his sporting
prints and model-car collection, and she
could display her favorite artwork, dried
flowers, and assorted treasures from her past.

The house was not large, so they weren't
sure how to accomplish their goal. There
were four bedrooms on the second floor: a
small one that served as a guest room,
Richard's 5-year-old daughter's room, their
bedroom, and a shared office. They'd been

considering adding on, but the construction
costs deterred them. I suggested that we take
the office and divide it into two smaller
rooms, one for each of them. These small
spaces would be adequate as "places of their
own." And if the house were ever put on the
market, it would be easy to remove the wall
between the two spaces and to return the
room to its original size and function.

As you can see from the drawings
(above), the remodeling to make the room
into two spaces was minor, leaving more dollars for adding character to the resulting
rooms. Both Richard and Joyce ended up
using their spaces for offices as well as sitting places. Richard kept his wood shutters
closed and created a denlike area, with dark
oak wainscoting, a TV, and a recliner.

Joyce, by contrast, had sheer drapes over
the windows, light-colored carpeting and a

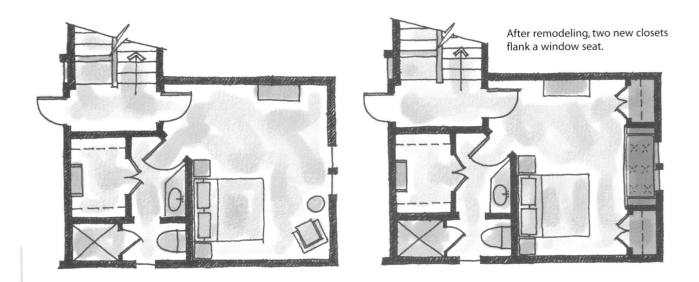

After remodeling, two new closets flank a window seat.

Closets create a window seat. Before remodeling, this spacious master bedroom was used only for sleeping.

pastel-colored couch. Her walls were covered with old photographs of relatives. Although she hadn't been planning this touch, a place of her own afforded her the opportunity to indulge her love of genealogy; she surrounded herself with images of those she was researching. After a few months with the arrangement, they both reported that they were happier, not only with the house but also with each other. All it had taken was a little creativity in rethinking what purpose each bedroom in the house might be put to.

Adding inward to create a window seat

Another client came to me with a deep longing for a window seat, something she had wanted since childhood. She envisioned a space with a beautiful view where she could curl up with a book and read in the afternoons before her children returned from school. Her husband had a woodshop in the basement that satisfied his need for a place of his own, but she had no equivalent. They considered adding a bay window and called me to help determine where it should be placed.

I pointed out that although a bay window can be beautiful, it might not be their best solution. A bay is not a good place to sit because it's not comfortable to lean against a window. A better solution is to have a solid wall perpendicular to a window that you can lean on while looking out. Because the master bedroom had ample floor area, a window seat could be added without building out by putting in closets on both sides of an existing window, creating an alcove (drawings above).

Flanking the window with 28-in.-deep closets and lowering the ceiling over the window created a passable window seat. The seat with drawers below for extra bedding

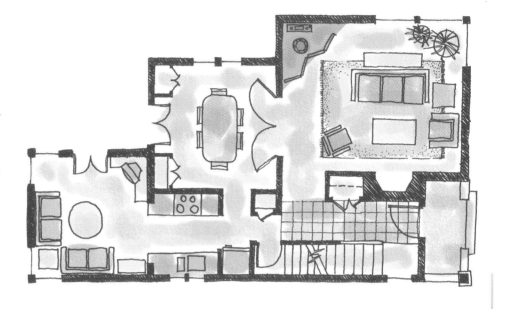

and a 4-in.-thick upholstered cushion made precisely for the kind of cozy, curl-up spot my client had been seeking. The total price of the remodel was reasonable, and the clients added some much-needed closet space to boot. Once again, adding on was avoided, and the available dollars could be spent instead on making the "place of one's own" really beautiful and comfortable.

The simplest approach

The final example of a place of one's own is the most economical of all and, in fact, is not really an architectural solution. It takes advantage of a spatial characteristic present in every room: the corner. My client was a meditator who wanted a place to accommodate his zafu (meditation cushion) and a low table for a few small objects that had meaning to him. But he did not want to have this area in the middle of a room used for other purposes. Rather, he wanted it to have a little privacy and separation from the other activities of the house. Unfortunately, the dollars available for this project were limited and wouldn't allow any moving of walls. So we came up with a creative solution using furniture rather than studs and

drywall. With the addition of a folding screen from a local imports store, we transformed a corner of the formal living room into a secluded place for meditation. The shape of the corner created a sense of shelter, and the screen provided a sense of enclosure (drawing above).

Over the years, I've designed places of one's own for all kinds of longings, from a location to practice calligraphy, to a writer's attic retreat, to an alcove for a friend to indulge her love of collage making. None of these places required a lot of space. In almost every case, if you are creative, you can find a small area that's rarely used in the house to make the place, without incurring the expense of adding on. Although these gestures seem small and perhaps insignificant, the effect such a space can have on your life is enormous.

A folding screen works, too. A four-panel folding screen creates a small, private meditation space in the corner of this living room.

It's human nature that we need places to be together and places to be apart.

Designing a Pantry

Have you noticed that when you start talking about storage, people light up? It's a subject near and dear to our hearts: where to put our stuff. And when it comes to food stuff, we become especially animated. So a pantry, for many folks, is the most important storage spot in the house.

But what constitutes a pantry? It can be anything from the bottom shelf in the linen closet to a spacious, cabinet-lined anteroom off the kitchen. Depending on the space available and the needs of the household, there is a variety of configurations possible.

This essay is devoted to a look at some of the most common pantry options. As you consider each, start with your own needs and habits to determine which one is most appropriate for you. The option that offers the greatest amount of storage may not always be the best choice, as you'll see.

For example, one of the most important things to understand about storage is that if something is not easily visible, it's less likely to be used. We all have different methods for remembering what we have and where we've stored it. Some people can have cans hidden away at the back of a dark shelf and still know exactly what's there. Others will buy something, put it on a shelf and forget it's there until the day they move, 20 years later. Clearly, the type of pantry that's appropriate for this person is different from the one that's right for the person with the infallible memory. As with everything in house design, the solution has to be tailored to the user.

The pantry closet

The simplest of all pantries is a basic closet lined with shelves (drawing facing page). It has a single access door, ideally with a light that turns on and off when the door is opened and closed. The advantage of this design is that when you open the door, you see everything with one sweep of the eye.

I normally make pantry shelves the depth of a cereal box—about 10 in., which can accommodate almost any kind of packaging. Some people will also use this kind of pantry to store occasional-use items, such as large

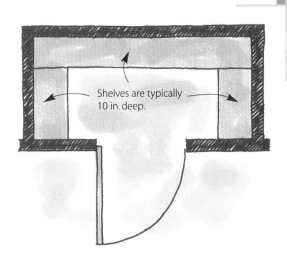

Shelves are typically 10 in. deep.

If you've got the room, a pantry closet is a good choice.
The pantry closet is not as space efficient as other designs, but it has major advantages when it comes to good visibility of stored items.

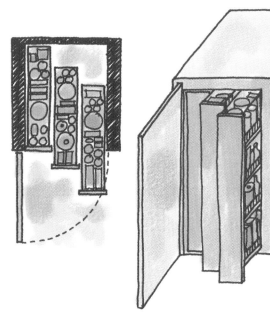

Achieving maximum storage. The pull-out pantry is an excellent choice when space is tight. Typical installations stretch from floor to ceiling.

platters and coffee urns. These items require deeper shelving that should be sized to fit.

Beware of the urge to fill the pantry closet with deep shelves to maximize space. Although you will have more shelf surface, you won't be able to see most of it easily, so you'll end up using only the front few inches of each shelf, reducing the effective storage capacity. It's counterintuitive, but it's true for most people.

Because the items stored in a pantry of this type are generally not needed every day, the pantry closet can be almost anywhere, from the basement (for those without mobility problems) to the mudroom.

The pull-out pantry

One of my favorites, a pull-out pantry uses every cubic inch of space for storage and can easily be worked into the main kitchen area (drawing right). Even devoting 1½ ft. of linear cabinet space to this type of storage can greatly increase the quantity of food you can keep close at hand. Typically,

each pull-out shelf is quite shallow, with room for one or two cans from front to back, and extends the standard 2-ft. depth of the countertop. The advantage of this design is that visibility is excellent. Pull out any one of the vertical drawers, and you can see everything in that drawer.

The disadvantage of this kind of pantry storage is that it is not designed for bulkier items like multiple rolls of toilet paper or paper towels. But if you can live with these

One of the most important things to understand about storage is that if something is not easily visible, it's less likely to be used.

items under the sink in the bathroom and laundry, there's no other pantry design I know of that will store so much in such a small area.

The fold-out pantry

Another popular design for a confined location is the fold-out pantry. Once again, every cubic inch can be put to use (drawing below). But in my experience, the fold-out pantry doesn't work as well as the pull-out variety. The common result is that the deeper recesses are accessed infrequently and thus contain forgotten items. If you choose this solution, open up all the folding shelves each week before you go grocery shopping to refresh your memory as to what items you already have.

The cabinet pantry

With kitchens becoming ever more expensive and showy, an increasingly common pantry style is one that sports the same cabinets as the kitchen. Although it can be beautiful to look at, this pantry approach is expensive and space-consuming, and often is far less convenient than the ideas I've already mentioned. Without stepped shelving, which allows the items in back to be raised for easier viewing, this style of pantry suffers from the same problem as regular kitchen cabinetry. The stuff in back disappears from view and from memory. If the shelves are deep, it's best to include some pull-out drawers inside so that you can access the items in the back.

The other drawback of this style of pantry is that you can see only a few items at a time: the ones behind that particular cabinet door. For the memory wizards, this isn't a problem, but for most of us, it can be a major frustration. Murphy's law ensures that the item you are looking for is behind the last door.

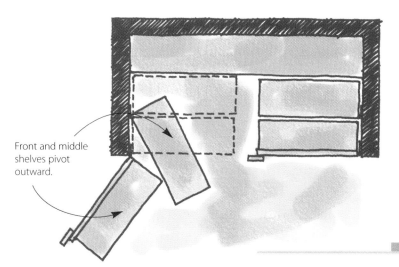

Front and middle shelves pivot outward.

Maximum storage with less convenience.
The fold-out pantry is compact, but items in the back can be forgotten if the shelves in front aren't folded out frequently.

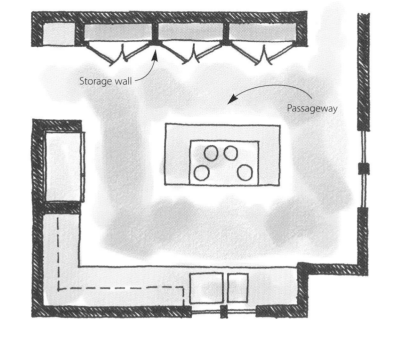

The hallway pantry

In attempting to make the most of a limited area, architects and interior designers are often pushed to come up with creative storage solutions. One of my favorites is the hallway pantry (drawing right). If you have a wall that defines one edge of a hallway or walkway, you can increase its width by 10 in. to 12 in. and add an efficient pantry that's perfectly suited for food storage. Designed to accommodate cereal boxes and anything smaller, you can line the hallway with shelves, either leaving them open or covering them with cabinet doors. If the walkway opens directly onto the kitchen, you may want to consider adding some glass doors so that you can see what's being stored inside while protecting the pantry from dust accumulation.

The stud-pocket pantry

Here's another suggestion that I developed during my college days. I'm sure it's not original, but if you haven't thought of it yourself, it may help. On the way to the basement of the house I was living in, there was a stud wall with no drywall on the side facing the stair. By adding horizontal cross members between studs, we were able to make some narrow shelves, 3½ in. deep, that were perfect for soup and tuna-fish cans. Although in a pantry like this one, the cereal box has to be placed sideways, it is adequate for most small-scale items. It's by no means a glorious solution, but it can work to alleviate the problems of a tiny kitchen.

This last solution illustrates another important point when designing almost anything. Don't let yourself become too constrained by notions of how something is "supposed" to be done. Frequently, the best solutions are arrived at by thinking outside the standard approach. So whatever your budget and whatever your needs, keep in mind that the most important criterion is whether the design helps you find what you are looking for when you need it. No matter how beautiful or clever a design, if it's not convenient for the person who uses it most frequently, it's not a good solution to the problem.

The hallway pantry. Adding a 10-in.-to-12-in. deep pantry storage wall along a hall or passageway can add a lot of storage in an efficient manner.

Planning Makes Recycling Easy

When I was in college, back in the 1970s, I wrote a paper entitled "But How Do We Get There From Here?" decrying the hopelessness of getting any significant percentage of the population to recycle. In the ensuing decades, I watched with incredulity as something I had imagined quite impossible happened. Only a few years later, most of my friends and neighbors were dutifully bringing their recyclables to the curb every couple of weeks for the regular curbside pick up. Now that recycling is a regular part of many of our lives though, I do have some suggestions for improvements to the process. And of course, it all starts in the designs of our homes.

Mastering the art of effortless recycling requires that you first become a keen observer of your household's waste-generation habits. In most residential areas today, we can recycle a wide variety of items, from the conventional metals, glass, and newspaper, to glossy paper and plastic. So it's important to determine which recycling receptacles are reasonably located in the kitchen, which can be located elsewhere, and which you don't need at all because they would rarely be used.

Locate receptacles close to the source

Most important in accommodating recycling receptacles is to locate them close to where the recyclable item is normally abandoned. In the case of newspapers, this may be the kitchen table or the couch in the family room, while for metals this may be adjacent to the kitchen sink. Any design that increases convenience makes recycling much more likely to become standard practice.

You should also consider the size of the receptacle for each recyclable. In many households, for example, there is far more glass storage required than metal storage. For others, it's the other way around. It makes sense to provide a secondary storage location, which could even be the curbside recycling bin itself (drawing facing page), for any item that requires a disproportionate amount of space.

> **Secondary storage ought to be convenient, too.**
> If you have only biweekly or monthly recycling pick-up, you may want a secondary staging area in the garage. A three-bin cart eases storage as well as hauling of recyclables to the curb.

2. Make a list of the items that are accepted by your recycling company. These normally include some or all of those listed here:
   - Newspapers
   - Catalogs and magazines
   - Cardboard
   - Plastic
   - Glass (which may be separated by color)
   - Metals (which may be separated by specific type)

3. Next to each category, indicate the items that your household typically generate; for example:
   - Metals

     –Aluminum cans—beer, soda
     –Steel cans—tuna fish, pet food

4. Estimate the quantity of waste in each category generated per two-week period. (This is often difficult to quantify if you aren't already recycling. You may want to conduct a test for a month to get a gauge on volume.)

5. Identify where each item is typically "abandoned." For example:
   - Beer cans: back deck and family room
   - Soda cans: family room and kitchen island
   - Tuna-fish cans: kitchen island
   - Pet-food cans: kitchen island

6. Determine the best location for a recycling station for each category.

Guidelines for recycling setup

The following is a checklist and questionnaire to help you determine some of the critical criteria for your household to help you design an effective recycling system for your home:

1. What is the recycling pick-up schedule for your locale? (Post this schedule somewhere so it's easy to refer to.)

Gather recyclables near their source.
A newspaper-stacking rack allows orderly storage as well as easy bundling and tying when full.

Note that if the items are typically thrown away in areas of the house that are far apart, it may make sense to designate two different recycling locations for this category of item. In the example above, if the kitchen were far removed from the family room, it might be appropriate to provide one metal receptacle in each room.

7. Investigate the types of recycling receptacles available to you. There are now many household organizing stores and catalogs, most of which offer a number of elegant solutions for recycling. Be wary of products that are too small to be useful however— I've recently noticed a focus on beauty at the expense of practicality. If you are planning to locate recycling containers within cabinetry, there are a lot of pull-out basket designs, a couple of which are illustrated here. A cabinet supplier can help you evaluate options.

8. Next, determine what kind of receptacle would be most convenient for each category of recyclable, and where such a receptacle might best be located. If you are remodeling, or simply moving furniture around to accommodate the new recycling containers, this will present different challenges obviously, than if you are designing from scratch, or adding on.

9. Think through the integration of the particular receptacle into the interior decor of the home so that it doesn't stick out like a sore thumb. For example, in my opinion, the best way to accommodate old newspapers is in a stackable rack. Locating this in the middle of the family room however may not be aesthetically acceptable. Is there a closet or cupboard nearby that could contain the newspaper rack? If not, could a screen or cabinet surround be made to hide the rack from view?

10. Evaluate the overall solution. In any design solution, once you've determined the solutions to each individual problem, it's important to take a step back and look at the overall solution. So once all the recyclable containers have been determined, look over the plan for all containers to check for inefficiencies. Are you missing something obvious? For example, would it be more sensible to combine the pull-outs for metal and glass, even though you generate more of one item than the other, so that you can use an off-the-shelf pull-out product with two baskets, rather than

Undercabinet solutions. There are many different one- and two-bin pull-outs available, both those you can install in an existing cabinet and those available from a cabinetmaker.

using two separate pull-outs of different sizes which will take up more cabinet space (drawing right)?

11. Think through the design of the secondary staging area. This may be no more than a recycling bin in the garage. But if you generate a lot of recyclables, you may want to look into a recycling cart with three or four recycling bins (available from most household organization catalogs). This will also make it easier to wheel to the curb if you have a longer driveway.

Although thinking through the design of the recycling system for your home may not be as glorious or aesthetically rewarding as some of the other aspects of house design, it can have a big impact on both livability and sustainability. There are few things we can do so easily that can have such a significant impact on consumption of natural resources.

The easier we make it for our household to recycle, the more they will do so, and in turn, the less waste we'll be shipping off to the landfill each week. It often amazes people to see how little trash they actually generate when they fully engage in the art of recycling.

And best of all, it doesn't have to be a burden or inconvenience at all. That's a sure sign of a good design solution. My skepticism of the 1970s has been solidly replaced by a confidence in our human ingenuity and will to look after our home—both residentially and planetarily.

Sources of Recycling Solutions

D&P Industries Inc.
www.urbangardencenter.com
(866) 560-4400

Get Organized!
www.shopgetorganized.com
(800) 803-9400

Organize Everything
www.organize-everything.com
(800) 600-9817

Real Goods
www.realgoods.com
(800) 762-7325

Recycled Plastics Marketing
www.rrpm.com
(425) 867-3200

Stacks and Stacks HomeWares
www.stacksandstacks.com
(877) 278-2257

It often amazes people to see how little trash they actually generate when they fully engage in the art of recycling.

FOUR

Attention to
Detail

When architects use the word *detail,* they mean how materials, shapes, and patterns come together to form an integrated design. It's primarily the details that make a well-designed object or room look and feel so pleasing. Yet, as I discovered when I started traveling around the country teaching about the Not So Big House, most nonarchitects only consider the colloquial usage of detail, which means something akin to "accessorizing." But as you will learn in this section, the word has far more depth and far-reaching effects.

A well-known architect of the twentieth century, Mies Van der Rohe, is famous for having said "God is in the details." It's a wonderful quote, but what does he mean exactly? When a number of different materials and forms are brought together for a specific purpose, and the resulting design appears effortless and beautiful, there's a transcendent quality to it. There's a "moreness" to it that is palpable, even though you'd be hard pressed to describe how or why it seems that way. That "moreness" comes from the care with which the materials and forms have been crafted by the designer.

If you look at the drawing on the facing page, you'll see how the materials composing this corner have been detailed to look absolutely natural. How else could it be? Yet there was an elaborate process undertaken to make it seem that way. To start with, window size had to be researched. And the exact beam size required to support the upper level had to be determined. The width of the beam then determined the width of the jamb (the wood spacer between the windows) so they would align perfectly, and the width of the widest standard window determined the difference in dimension between upper and lower levels. If someone hadn't spent the time to figure this out on paper, long before construction started, the result would never have appeared so effortless or elegant.

This section illustrates how this kind of thinking can dramatically improve the quality and character of a home. Whether you are sculpting the shape of a space with ceiling height variations, or doing something as seemingly mundane as locating a smoke alarm, when you pay careful attention to each of these details, you'll find that it's not so difficult to attain that quality of "moreness."

Understanding the Effects of Ceiling Height

H ave you noticed that most of the words we use in English to describe spatial interest have to do with size and height? We talk about spacious living rooms, vaulted or cathedral ceilings, broad expanses of wall or window. Our language encourages us to believe that all these attributes make a place better. It isn't true.

It is not the height of the ceilings that makes a house more or less interesting, but rather the variation in ceiling height. A house with 10-ft. ceilings in every room can be just as boring as one with 8-ft. ceilings throughout. With so many new homes going up around the country that have 10-ft. ceilings in most rooms and cathedral ceilings in the main living spaces, it is gradually dawning on us that perhaps these tall ceilings are not all they're cracked up to be. They look good in the real-estate ads in the newspaper, but the reality is that these tall rooms are not easy to live in. They don't encourage settling in, and their inhabitants often find themselves huddling in a corner of the kitchen,

Designing tranquillity.
The lowered ceiling in this ingle-nook creates a sense of intimacy. In general, smaller spaces require lower ceilings for comfort.

trying to find a cozy spot in which to socialize. Meanwhile, the cathedral-ceilinged living room sits unoccupied, waiting for a few dozen friends to bring it into proportion. The biases of our language have literally talked us into something that impresses rather than nurtures.

What kind of space appeals to you?

One of the first things I recommend to my clients as they plan a new home or addition is that they take note of the places they visit that really make them feel at home. You can do this by visiting your friends' houses, model homes, open houses on real-estate tours, and, in some areas, architectural tours. Be sure to include some older homes in your research as well as newer ones. And don't forget to take a tape measure with you. Check out not only the horizontal dimensions of the spaces you like but also the vertical dimensions.

As you go about your daily routine, notice which places attract you the most. Are you the kind of person who likes to sit in the corner with your back sheltered by the wall, or are you more likely to sit in the middle of the room?

If you have an opportunity to visit an architecturally designed home, you'll often find that the ceiling height of each space

Vary ceiling heights to distinguish spaces.
In this house, lowered soffits and floating shelves help define spaces without the use of walls. The main ceiling height is 8 ft., but it seems taller in contrast to the lowered ceiling elements.

Take away the variations in ceiling height, and the identities of the individual spaces are seriously reduced.

Soffits make good borders.
The dropped portions of the ceiling around the border of this kitchen give the room a sheltered feel. Called soffits, these lower ceilings are also convenient places to install recessed light fixtures.

oped no language for the feelings evoked by taller and shorter ceiling heights, we don't know how to ask for the variety shown in these illustrations. Yet such sculpting of the space can have an enormous impact on the livability of a home. Here are some simple ceiling-height strategies that you can use in a home—new or existing—to tailor each space to its activity.

1. **Soffits lower the edges of a ceiling.** A room of almost any height can be made more intimate with the introduction of a soffit or shelf above window height, either along one wall or all around the room (drawing left). For someone fearful that a space will feel too small, this strategy offers the benefits of higher ceilings in the center of a room, with the comfort and shelter of lowered ceilings at the room's periphery. This strategy is similar to the effect of wearing a wide-brimmed hat. We can watch the world from below the brim while remaining sheltered. Soffits do very much the same thing.

2. **Lower the ceilings in smaller areas.** If you have an alcove off a room or a window seat, lowering the ceiling in that area tends to define it more strongly as its own place, even if it is quite small. In our example (drawing facing page, top left), the library alcove feels like a separate space because of the 6-ft. 10½-in. ceiling. Many people are afraid of making a ceiling any lower than 8 ft., yet there is something

varies with the function and proportion of each space. Lower ceilings are typical in smaller spaces, and taller ceilings in larger areas. Alcoves such as window seats, piano niches, and fireplace inglenooks are often made lower to shelter the activity within (drawing p. 88), and the more formal spaces such as the dining room and the living room are made taller to increase the sense of ceremony. A low ceiling in a large room can feel quite oppressive, while a tall ceiling in a tiny room can feel almost intimidating—like standing at the bottom of an elevator shaft.

By varying ceiling heights (drawings p. 89), you can distinguish one space from another without obstructing views with walls. But take away the ceiling-height variety, and lo and behold, you have just another homogenized space. Because we have devel-

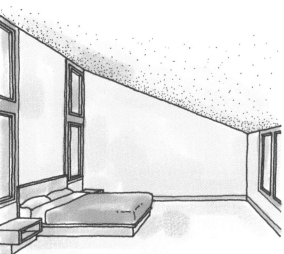

Lower ceilings form alcoves.
This library alcove works as such because of the lowered ceiling. If the ceiling were the same height as the rest of the room, the table and chairs would be much less inviting.

A floating shelf can help.
A common problem in many newer houses is a sloped ceiling, such as this one. With no shelter over the bed, this space can be uncomfortable for some people.

appealing about having spaces that invite you to sit down, as this one does. And lowered ceilings accentuate the height of adjacent spaces, making them seem taller by contrast.

3. **Counterbalance a sloped ceiling with a floating shelf.** A room with a ceiling sloped in only one direction is one of the most awkward spaces to inhabit comfortably, yet it is a space often found in newer homes (drawings right). If you lie on a bed or sit on a couch placed against a shorter wall, your eye is drawn upward. But there is no resolution. You are simply looking up into a tight corner of space, with a vast expanse of wall staring back at you. If, on the other hand, you put the furniture against the taller wall, there is almost a sense of reverse vertigo. It's not a pleasant situation, and these types of rooms frequently remain unused.

By adding a floating shelf above the bed, the sense of shelter is greatly increased.

It is not the height of the ceilings that makes a house more or less interesting, but rather the variation in ceiling height.

A simple solution is to add a floating shelf along the tall wall at the height of the opposite wall. This brings the room height down over the sitting area without affecting the overall height of the room.

4. **Use the space near the eaves.** Because of our mistrust of low ceilings, we tend to ignore the space under 8 ft. in houses where the rooms are directly under the roof (drawing below). But if we consider using this space, we find that rooms can be both larger and more intimate. The sloped ceiling adds significant character to the room and creates a cocoon of sorts for a bed or for a comfortable chair.

To really appreciate the effect of ceiling height on our lives, look through any magazine on home design, and you'll see a fantastic variety of ceiling shapes, forms, and heights. The trick is to remember that both the camera lens and our language tend to favor the taller-and-bigger-is-better worldview, while our bodies actually favor something a little more human in scale. Focusing more attention on the contrast between one ceiling and another—and less on the overall ceiling height—will give us homes that are both more comfortable and more livable.

Get the most from the space under the roof. Many newer homes ignore the angled-ceiling space under the roof and simply end the room at the point where the ceiling drops below 8 ft. But such space can enhance both the room's size and its charm.

Using Tile
to Personalize
a Kitchen or
Bathroom

I took part in an interview for an article about "timeless design." Focusing on kitchens and bathrooms, the interviewer wanted to know exactly what makes a design age gracefully. I was the last of four people to be consulted. The other three all had suggested that timeless means low key, preferably white. But to me, timeless means something different. I see so much design today that becomes downright bland in its attempt to be inoffensive. Far from being something that anyone would want to preserve, it is quickly torn out and replaced by something with character.

Tile can be used to create something beautiful, memorable, and, indeed, timeless. Simple features, such as a careful composition of tile at a kitchen backsplash or in a tub enclosure, can give not just that room but the whole house a quality that endears it to its owners. Tile is easy to make a statement with, even for those not trained in design. Whether you are working with an architect or designer or doing the design work yourself, tile presents an opportunity to make a big impact with only a small investment of time and money.

So many tile choices, and so many places to use it

Tile options are so extensive today that people often are overwhelmed. Prices can vary dramatically—from $2.50 per square foot for standard wall tile to $200 per square foot for handmade works of art. I've seen clients labor over the decision, often selecting something safe because they could not decide on anything else. Others pick the most expensive tile in hopes the price somehow guarantees good results.

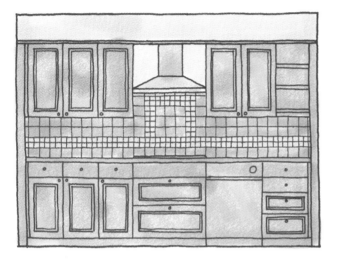

But tile itself, no matter what the cost, is only a small piece of the design process. If my clients are concerned about cost, I suggest they select inexpensive tiles that come in a variety of colors and arrange them in a design. If money is not a big concern, I suggest selecting a line with some beautiful feature tiles, which offer plenty of inspiration for a design that will enhance the character of a room.

In houses old and new, tile typically is used at the kitchen backsplash; sometimes on the kitchen floor, and bathroom floors, tub and shower surrounds, and bathroom-sink backsplashes; and sometimes even on bathroom walls. Before selecting a tile style, I normally begin by looking at these areas to determine exactly where I want tile to go and whether these areas lend themselves to a particular type of design. Choosing a design direction before selecting the tile narrows the possibilities and makes selection a little easier.

Selecting a focal point

Tile helps create a focal point in a room, and it should resonate with the area you select. Generally, there is more than one spot in a room that is conducive to being a natural focal point. In a kitchen, for example, there is the cooktop, the sink area, and the breakfast bar, to name a few. Depending on your budget, all of these areas can be tiled, creating a multitude of harmonious focal points, or one can be made to stand out.

Tile can also be used in less obvious ways and areas. For a kitchen sink with a window above, you might consider framing the window in tile rather than wood or maybe running a line of tile around the wood that trims the window.

On one recent bathroom remodel, the clients knew they wanted to replace the carpet on the floor with tile. They also wanted to give the room some character. Because the

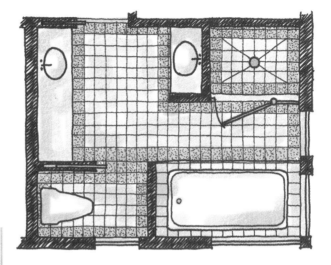

room was not large, we decided that we would use smaller tile so that we could create a border around the fixtures in the room (drawing right).

You don't need to apply tile to every available surface. One of my favorite details is to run a single line of tile along a backsplash and trim this line off with a wood cap that's just wide enough to hold spice bottles. You can then run the trim line up each side of the tile area behind the cooktop to frame it.

This backsplash detail also works very well in bathrooms. I often run a tile line around the room at the same height, capping the bottom and top of the tile in the same way. Alternately, running a tile band alone around the room at this height gives a wainscoted effect with no need to apply tile or wood below it if it doesn't suit your style or budget. Using a different color of paint above the tile and below it gives the same effect.

Generating a design strategy

After identifying the focal area of the room, it's helpful to draw all the surfaces to be tiled on grid paper and try out some different design ideas. I usually try to echo some aspect of the focal design in other areas of the room, as can be seen in the kitchen backsplash drawings. And I'll often do three or four designs before settling on the one I like the best.

Simple patterns make a big impact. Tile choices can be overwhelming, so concentrating on one area and choosing one design direction help to narrow the field. Here, a bathroom benefited from small floor tiles with contrasting borders around the fixtures.

Use inexpensive tile creatively. For a great look on a budget, you can tile the entire backsplash. You don't need to use expensive tile. In this drawing, standard 6x6 tiles in two colors make an interesting design without costing a lot.

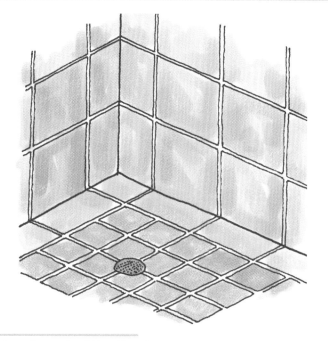

Grout joints should be aligned.
Two sizes of tile in a shower look neat and tailored when grout lines meet. In this shower, a half-width of 8x8 wall tile has been used to create a border for 4x4 floor tile.

To ensure a design that works, it's important you have the dimensions drawn accurately. The distance between the counter and upper cabinets in the kitchen, for example, can strongly affect which design strategy looks best. I try to avoid designing in tile cuts except at the ends of walls, or where tiles meet the counter or the upper cabinet surfaces. Having partial tiles in a design can look like a mistake unless it's very well executed.

Thinking in color

Once I've selected the design strategy I like the most, I'll make five or six copies of my grid paper drawing, then get out some colored pencils and play with color combinations. Although it's nearly impossible to get accurate representations of the available tile colors, it is usually possible to get close at least. When I've worked with clients who have difficulty envisioning color combinations, I'll sometimes take them to the tile showroom and layout a small segment of the proposed tile design with the showroom samples.

Careful alignments require planning

The manner in which tile is aligned will also influence the look of a design. If you use tile on the walls of a bathroom, for example, try to align grout joints between wall and floor tile. This touch gives the room a much more planned and finished look. You can either use the same size tile on wall and floor, or go to a larger tile on the floor. If you do use different-size tiles on the floor and walls, be sure to check that sizes are compatible. Just because a tile is labeled 4×4 doesn't mean the grout joints will align with those of an 8×8 tile from another company. It is for this reason that I usually try to stay with the same manufacturer if I'm trying to align tiles from one surface to another.

In a shower, you may want to use smaller tiles on the floor than on the wall. With more frequent grout joints, smaller tiles are

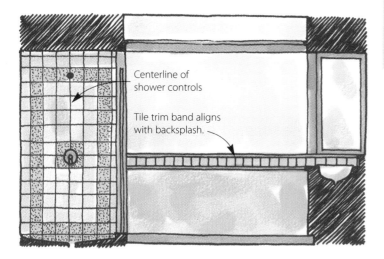

Centerline of
shower controls

Tile trim band aligns
with backsplash.

**Listening to what the
eye says.**
The tile pattern in the shower
should be centered on the
shower controls and shower
head, not on the shower
width. Because the eye is
sensitive to alignment, it is
better to line up tile patterns
around the centerlines of
these objects.

less slippery. I like to bring the wall tile
down to the floor and continue this size and
pattern for one more border row before
changing to smaller tile (drawing facing
page). Again, it gives a more tailored look,
and it also makes it easier for the tile layer to
align the drain with the tile pattern.

Other alignments to consider

One thing that can dramatically affect
the overall look and feel of a bathroom
is the alignment of tile with objects that
already decorate the walls and the floor. In a
shower, for example, one wall usually has
the shower controls and the shower head.
On a different wall, there will often be an
indented area for soap and shampoo. It
looks so much better when each of these
elements is aligned in some way with the
tile pattern.

I usually ask the plumber to align controls, shower head, and floor drain, and then
ask the tile installer to arrange his layout so
that the vertical axis though these elements
falls at the centerline of a tile.

Even with accurate drawings, it's important to review your design with the tile installer. He or she may not understand your
intentions perfectly, and sometimes, due to
the idiosyncrasies of a particular tile, the
spacing may need to be slightly different
from what you had envisioned. Also, in
some rooms, there may be more than one
visual cue to which tiles could be aligned.

Although most installers are careful to
center tiles with respect to the room or wall,
people are much more attuned to centering
with respect to objects on a wall. The question always is, "Centered on what?" I favor
centering on what the eye notices first
(drawing above).

I'll often make a list of "regulating principles" as well as the drawing, just to be clear about my intentions. In the drawing above, for example, the regulating principles would be:

- Focal design above cooktop to be aligned with center line of hood

- On either side of focal tile design, feature color tiles to be every other tile.

- If feature color tile falls at corner, other segment of feature tile to wrap

corner and appear on adjacent perpendicular wall.

Although it is often helpful to work with an interior designer or architect when designing special room features such as the kitchen backsplash or shower stall, there's no reason you can't do something highly creative by yourself. With careful measuring, you can design your own tile composition and build into your home a feature that enlivens and personalizes it for many years to come.

I see so much design today that becomes downright bland in its attempt to be inoffensive. Far from being something that anyone would want to preserve, it is quickly torn out and replaced by something with character.

Designing a Window Seat

I've loved window seats ever since I was a kid. There's something wonderful about sitting in a place situated between inside and out—a place that, while you are there, is just yours to enjoy.

Over the years I've discovered that I am not alone in this love. When I speak with clients about the possibility of adding a window seat here or there in their new house or remodeling, the suggestion is usually met with delight. It seems that because window seats are not strictly speaking a functional necessity, they've largely fallen out of favor over the past century. With the current enthusiasm for repersonalizing one's home, however, the window seat is experiencing a comeback. But just calling a place a window seat doesn't automatically make it a great place to be. There are a few guidelines to window seat design that can optimize the expense while creating a favorite spot.

How will you use your window seat?

One of the first steps when designing a window seat is to determine it's primary use or uses. For example:

- A place to curl up with a good book
- A place to look out at the view
- A place to sit and meditate
- A place for kids to play
- A place for overnight guests to sleep

Different purposes require different dimensions. For example, if the window seat is to be used as a bed, it has to accommodate the appropriate-size mattress. If the window seat is to be used for sitting, you'll need to consider not only the dimensions of the

There's something wonderful about sitting in a place situated between inside and out—a place that, while you are there, is just yours to enjoy.

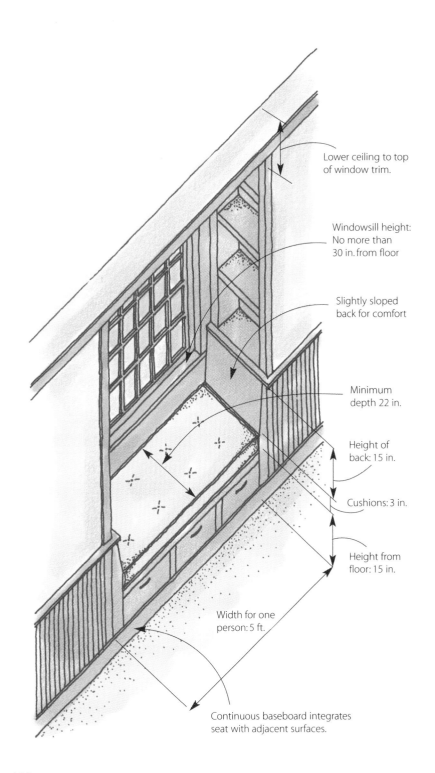

Lower ceiling to top
of window trim.

Windowsill height:
No more than
30 in. from floor

Slightly sloped
back for comfort

Minimum
depth 22 in.

Height of
back: 15 in.

Cushions: 3 in.

Height from
floor: 15 in.

Width for one
person: 5 ft.

Continuous baseboard integrates
seat with adjacent surfaces.

sitting surface but also back support—a
design feature that is frequently overlooked.

Comfort is in the proportions

As with so many aspects of house design,
the most important characteristics of
a well-designed window seat are its proportions. If it's too small, it won't be comfortable. If it's too big for the room, it can make
you feel like you're on display. If it's too low
in relation to the window, you won't be able
to see the views easily. By employing the
following guidelines you'll be able to avoid
these pitfalls.

1. **Depth from front to back.** If you are
   planning to sit with your feet up, and lean
   against one or other side, as is typically
   the case, the bare minimum from front
   to back is 22 in. to 24 in. Any less than
   this and you feel perched as opposed to
   settled (drawing left).

   If you have the room, a better depth
   for this sitting configuration is 30 in. to
   36 in. This gives you the space to spread
   out a bit, sit cross legged or tuck your
   legs to the side, still with room to spare.

   If children will also be using this area
   for playing, 36 in. or more is ideal. A few
   years ago I designed a 40-in.-deep window
   seat in a family room, and it essentially
   became the kids' playroom for a few years.
   They made it into their house within a
   house, and kept all their favorite toys

there, which had the added benefit of keeping the rest of the family room relatively toy free.

If the window seat will double as a bed, and if you plan to use a standard mattress in lieu of custom upholstery, make sure you get the exact dimensions of the mattress—both width and length—before construction begins. An inch too small in either direction and the functionality of the space will be greatly compromised. Although you can have a special cushion made to fit, standard sheets and blankets may not work.

2. **Width from side to side.** Width is typically a less critical dimension in terms of comfort. If you are designing a window seat for one, keep the width under 5 ft. so that it has a cozy feel to it. You can go as small as 3 ft. 6 in. wide and still have a workable window seat, though it will feel very different—more like a nest than a seat, requiring that you sit cross legged, or with feet propped against the adjacent wall.

Often the width of a window seat is regulated by the width of the group of windows it sits below. I usually make the window seat about 1 ft. wider than the window to allow for window trim on either side. Then I'll fill in the space to the adjacent walls with book shelves or closets, which allows you to easily create a window seat without the added expense of bumping out beyond the rectangular building envelope (drawing p. 103).

3. **Height off the floor.** Most people are very sensitive to the heights of chairs and couches, and the same holds true for window seats. Make it just an inch or two too high and it will not get used much. For most situations, 15 in. seems to be ideal. This allows for the addition of a 3-in.-thick upholstered cushion, while still maintaining the comfort range.

Before settling on the perfect height, test out some bench seats if you can, and see what feels best to you. Remember that in most cases a window seat isn't used like a chair. It's rare that you'll sit with your feet on the ground, because from this position you won't be able to see out of the window. So the seat surface can be a little lower than is normal for a chair, making it easy to plop down on. The implied invitation to sit seems to decrease with added height. But if the bench surface is too low, it will start to feel more like a step and less like a place to sit.

One final consideration—if you have an area where you'd like a window seat, but the window is too high for the seat-height recommendations, you can add a step up to the seat (drawing p. 102). The relationship between the windowsill and the seat surface is more important than the height of the seat above the floor.

4. **Height of the windowsill.** There's nothing more frustrating than a window seat where the window is too high to see out comfortably. If you think back to childhood you'll probably remember this experience—everything was designed for the adult-height view and you were too short to see out properly.

So the height of the windowsill becomes extremely important to a successful window seat design. In a new house or addition I try to place the windowsill about 2 ft. off the floor. The window seat then appears to be an integral part of the

Step up to the window seat.
If the window is 3 ft. or more above the floor, raise the seat 6 in. to 12 in. below the window and add a step.

window design, much like a wide surrounding frame. If you don't want to see this much window from the outside, you can go as high as 30 in. from floor to sill and still have excellent views from the seat. At 3 ft., though, you start to lose the sense of connection with the outdoors. Heights of 3 ft. or more work only if you add a step and make the seat surface higher, as described above (drawing left).

5. **Designing the leaning surface.** The most comfortable window seats have gently sloping sides, so that it's easy to lean back and feel supported. If the sloped back isn't a possibility, make sure there are plenty of cushions available so that you can create your own comfortable support. And also make sure there's at least one side of the window seat that has a leaning surface that extends 15 in. up from the bench top. If the space will be used for reading, I often add bookshelves above the leaning surface, which gives the area its own unique character.

6. **Height of the window-seat ceiling.** Ceiling height is less critical than the others in terms of function, but it can add a lot to the ambiance. If the window seat ceiling is slightly lower than the surrounding ceiling, the area will take on a nestlike quality, which for many window seat lovers is the desired effect. You can also arch the ceiling or drop it down to the height of the window trim—my personal favorite (drawing p. 100).

Without a change in ceiling height, the window seat is perceived as a continuation of the room and is less distinctly its own place. Although elegant in a photograph, these window seats tend to be less inviting in reality and thus get less use.

A window seat can be used for storage

When building a window seat, many people want to make use of the area below for storage. If you've got the budget for drawers below, by all means add them, but keep in mind that these are a cabinetry item and add significantly to the cost. There's not a lot of usable space given the low height of the bench seat, so it ends up being very expensive storage space that isn't terribly useful.

Another alternative is to fit the bench with a lift-up lid, providing access to the space below. If you plan to add a cushion, though, the lid will rarely be opened. And in some cases, a cushion is never made, and then no one sits on the window seat because it's not comfortable. Don't let a secondary use spoil what you set out to do in the first place—create a window seat.

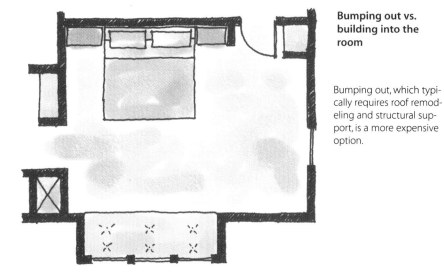

Bumping out vs. building into the room

Bumping out, which typically requires roof remodeling and structural support, is a more expensive option.

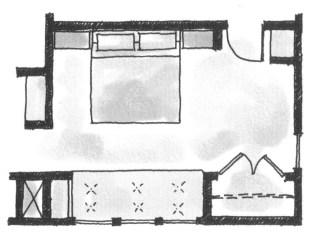

A less-expensive alternative is tucking a window seat between added bookshelves or closets at an existing window, which requires no exterior work.

With the current enthusiasm for repersonalizing one's home, the window seat is experiencing a comeback.

FIVE

Lighting
That Works

There are few things that affect us as much as access to light. The first house I owned was built in the late Victorian era when windows were used sparingly, direct exposure to sunlight was limited as much as possible, and artificial (man-made) lighting fixtures were provided only at the centers of ceilings, giving every room a homogeneous, surgical look. It was particularly gloomy in the winter.

After 10 such winters, I moved into a house I designed for myself, where I had implemented many of the lighting techniques described in this section. Goodbye gloom. Because I now lived in a house filled with natural light during the day, and with carefully designed artificial lighting for the evening hours, I never felt light deprived.

Sadly, most houses are rarely designed with good lighting in mind. Windows are set unceremoniously into walls, with little if any consideration given to how to maximize the amount of light that enters. Skylights, which can provide wonderful lighting when positioned properly, are usually just plunked onto the roof surface, with no thought given to how they will look from inside, what views they will provide, and what quantity of light they will reflect into the interior. And artificial lighting, one of the last things to be installed during the construction process, frequently gets short shrift because the budget has already been blown and there's almost no money left for light fixtures.

Most families use their houses more in the evening than any other time, so it makes sense to plan good lighting thoughtfully and to dedicate the necessary resources to making it work. Good lighting can dramatically enhance the ambiance of a home and create different moods for the various activities that take place in each room. Surprisingly, good lighting doesn't have to cost an arm and a leg either. It simply requires that you understand which fixtures perform which functions, and which one is best suited to the purpose you are putting it to.

Whether you're designing from scratch or remodeling, with a little attention given to how light enters, how it's reflected deeper into each space, and how each room is enhanced in the evening hours with appropriately located light fixtures, you can make your home a place of rejuvenation and radiance—literally.

Window Placement

We are light-sensitive creatures who tend to feel better about ourselves and our world when we have access to natural daylight. As with so much in this world, we have come to believe that if a little is good, a lot must be better. Ask anyone who has lived in a house made almost entirely of glass though, and they will tell you that there is a need for a happy medium. Too much light can cause a sense of agoraphobia, with no place to nestle. Since windows are the most expensive component of a home's exterior, when considered on a per square foot basis, wouldn't it be a good idea to make every window really enhance the experience of living in the house? To understand how to make the most of each window, we need to look at how and where windows work.

1. **A passage for air, light, and view**. For centuries, windows were simply holes in the wall, a means for exchanging the stagnant and smoke-filled air of the interior with fresh air from outside. Up until the early part of the last century, every window was custom made for the particular opening in the wall and was typically made by local craftspeople. It's only been in the last few decades that windows have been mass-produced, and new manufacturing technology has made them less drafty and more affordable. Although they're primarily valued for aesthetic reasons in modern times, they still function to let air in and out of a home, which is just as important today as in the past.

2. **Contrast between areas of many windows and areas of few**. By recognizing that we need both bright places and more sheltered places for comfort, we start to understand one of the primary concepts in window placement. Part of what makes

We are light-sensitive creatures who tend to feel better about ourselves and our world when we have access to natural daylight.

Thick walls are reflectors, too. Delicate patterns of light and shadow through multipane windows are a hallmark of stone-walled European cottages.

a window such a desirable feature is the contrast it creates with the solid wall surfaces that surround it.

As you think about the composition of a house from the perspective of interior needs, make sure that you include both light-filled places and places with fewer windows that have a more introverted nature. For example, the light-filled place might be the sunroom or the main living space in the house, while the darker place might be a library, den, or even a bedroom—a place that is perhaps lined with bookshelves, or paneling, with only one or two smaller windows set among the shelves (drawings above and p. 110).

3. **Light on two sides of every room**. For readers familiar with the book *A Pattern Language,* by Christopher Alexander et al. (Oxford University Press, 1977), you'll recognize this concept from one of the patterns in the book. When a room has windows on two different walls, the whole space seems to come alive. People within such a space look healthier and more alert, and objects within the room take on a richer texture and character. Why is this? Think for a moment of a room with only one electric light in it. The objects in the room are described for our eye only by that one source of light, and the room takes on a two-dimensional, static quality. When an additional light source is introduced in another part of

Moving the window away from the corner creates a shadow zone.
You can manipulate the amount of daylight that is coming into a room by placing a window closer to or farther from a light-colored wall surface.

the room, each object springs to three-dimensional life because our eye now receives more information from light reflecting off various surfaces from different angles. The same rules hold true with windows. Each window can be thought of as a light source, and when daylight enters a room from multiple directions, we receive more visual input.

4. **Reflecting light off walls and ceiling.** To enhance the number of directions by which light enters a room, you can actually use wall and ceiling surfaces as reflectors (drawings above). The drawing on the left shows a window located directly adjacent to a perpendicular wall surface. Daylight enters through the window, bounces off the wall surface, and lights objects within the room from a different angle from that of the direct rays from the sun. Positioning a window in this way also tends to blur

the distinction between interior and exterior. The bright interior wall surface perpendicular to the window is almost as bright as the outside world, and there is no apparent obstacle between inside and out. As the window is moved away from the adjacent perpendicular wall, as seen in the drawing at right, a dark area is formed. Less light is reflected into the room, and the distinction between inside and out is more exaggerated.

This concept also explains why many people like the look and feel of a house with thick walls, such as are common in adobe structures and in stone cottages in Europe and the Middle East. The thickness of the wall acts as a reflector frame surrounding each window, bouncing light around the room from many directions (drawing p. 107).

Think of windows as an opportunity to personalize a house.
By creating patterns with windows, you can give a house a distinct look. But be judicious. If the windows don't share some common shapes and patterns, the exterior of the house can become a jumbled mess.

5. **Window patterns**. Window units can also be combined into a graphic composition of sorts. The most common combinations are sets of ganged windows, typically two or three together, though many other placements are possible. Most architects use this concept of window composition to add personality to a home. Whether thinking about this composition from inside the space or from outside the house, window patterns can greatly enhance its look and feel.

Our imaginations and our budgets are the only things limiting what is possible when it comes to window patterns. The drawings above offer ideas that I find particularly appealing. One thing to avoid, however, is giving each room a different pattern. Try to work within a theme, either using a number of similar patterns, or a single primary window pattern in the main living space, and simpler, more standard configurations throughout the rest of the house. Like a good poem, the overall composition of the house can benefit from both creativity, and restraint.

The connection between interior spaces, exterior views, and direct sunlight can enormously enhance the experience of living in a home.

Use bookshelves to surround windows. Bookshelves can be used to create a thick wall appearance when they surround windows in a study, den, or library.

6. Relating to the great outdoors

Finally, and most obviously, it is important to locate windows to take advantage of the views and special features of a building site. It is amazing to me how often a house turns a blind face toward a spectacular view or to southern light. The connection between interior spaces, exterior views, and direct sunlight can enormously enhance the experience of living in a home. It doesn't even have to cost more money. All that is required is a little forethought to recognize the orientation of the house, the views to be taken in, and where these will fall with respect to planned seating areas.

It is so obvious when you spend time in a house that has been given this kind of attention in the planning process. You sit down at the breakfast table, for example, and you're presented with a view of a lovely maple tree in the corner of the backyard; or you take a seat in the main living area, and you're greeted by a south-facing window that looks onto a rolling hillside with a glimpse of a lake beyond. Even if you don't have any particularly special site characteristics, placing a bird feeder or flowering bush in a place where it can be enjoyed from inside will go a long way in increasing the enjoyment of a house by its inhabitants.

How to Use Skylights for Maximum Effect

In the search for a lighter, brighter house, many homeowners assume that a generous sprinkling of skylights will help. After all, if one is good, more must be better. But often, this approach brings with it a host of unanticipated problems that could have been avoided with a little more care in placement. So I'd like to propose a systematic approach to skylight location. It's important to start by evaluating whether a skylight is really the best solution for a particular situation, and then evaluate where to locate the skylight to maximize the amount of light it introduces into a space.

Many skylight lovers have come from houses that are very dark, and they tend to overcompensate as a result.

Skylight pros and cons

Skylights do some things that windows just can't do. They allow light into areas that lack an exterior wall, and they can offer light in rooms that require all wall surfaces for storage, such as a closet. And they can generally increase the quantity of daylight available in a space.

There are some things to take into consideration, however. The most common concern about skylights is leaking. A skylight will not leak unless it has been installed improperly, which is a common occurrence, or unless the unit is defective, which is rare. So the key to getting a skylight that doesn't leak is to hire someone who understands the principles of proper flashing and who knows how to follow the instructions that come with the skylight.

Another problem common to skylights is overheating, especially in warmer climates. Skylights on the south or west side of a roof in a warm climate can make the rooms they

Skylight wells are as important as the skylight. A skylight, installed the typical way on the left side of the drawing, penetrates the roof with a straight-sided skylight well. But when the sidewalls of the shaft are flared, as on the right, the amount of light entering the room is increased dramatically.

open into almost unusable when the sun is shining on a cloudless day.

In colder climates, skylights can contribute significantly to heat loss in winter months. A skylight is only slightly more insulating than a hole in the roof with a piece of corrugated cardboard across it. When the skylight is surrounded by roofing materials with an insulation value of R-40 or better, warm interior air makes a beeline for the cool skylight, condenses on its surface and causes either dripping, which is often assumed to be leaking, or unsightly stains on the adjacent drywall. Although both of these problems can be solved with adequate air movement around the skylight, there is still some question about the advisability of a hole in the roof in the first place.

Is a skylight the answer?

My own approach to skylight use and location is first to see if the job can be done with a window. So when clients tell me they love skylights and want to include them wherever possible in their new home or remodel, I try to find out what it is that attracts them. For a few, it is to increase the sense that they are outside. When surrounding views are spectacular and the climate relatively benign, this situation may be an appropriate use of multiple skylights. But for most, it is the desire for a lot of natural light. Many skylight lovers have come from houses that are very dark, and they tend to overcompensate as a result. In this case, windows will usually work just as well, but without the additional heat loss or gain. If a window won't work, I'll consider a skylight or two. Like real estate, location is the secret.

I try to avoid broad areas of skylights, given the associated heating and cooling challenges. If you have a set of windows lighting a space, the additional light provided by skylights is often extraneous. On the other hand, in a room where it is difficult to get adequate daylight from windows, a skylight may be an ideal solution.

Put the skylight in the right place

When the well meets the wall. In this tub enclosure, you can see the effect of aligning the lower edge of the skylight well with the exterior wall of this bath alcove. The entire wall becomes the skylight's reflector surface. Notice that the two segments of sloped ceiling on each side of the skylight shaft are dark by contrast.

Where a skylight is placed in relation to surrounding walls and ceiling is crucial. Proper location of one skylight provides more light in a room than two or three that are installed the conventional way.

Let's look at two typical skylight locations and how they affect the light in a room. In a room that has a section of sloped ceiling, as in the illustration (drawing on the facing page), the typical approach is to place the skylight more or less in the middle of the sloped surface. The sidewalls of the skylight opening are at 90° to the slope of the ceiling. This placement creates a square of light almost exactly the size of the skylight itself. If you visualize this, you'll see that the sidewalls of the opening are bright and bounce light into the room. They function like reflectors on a light fixture.

What if you were able to make those sidewalls larger? The result would be larger reflectors, and so more light. It isn't hard to do this. All you have to do is to change the location of the skylight slightly and to alter the angle of the sidewalls (drawing on the facing page). These two surfaces provide a much greater reflector area and so bring much more usable light into the room.

If the skylight is directly adjacent to a sidewall of the room itself, as in the drawing of the bathtub alcove (drawing above), you get the most light possible from the skylight. Not only does it serve its purpose more effectively, but it also looks beautiful.

We can apply this same enlarged-reflector concept for another common skylight application: in the middle of a room with a flat ceiling (drawings p. 114) where light is needed over a kitchen island or other work surface. If you make a vertical shaft from the roof to the flat ceiling below, the surface area of that shaft is limited, and the opening to the room can end up smaller than the skylight. If the walls of the shaft are flared, however, there is greater surface area to reflect daylight, and the opening to the room is significantly larger. Often, the structure of the roof—trusses, for example—prevents you

Vertical and flared skylight wells in a trussed roof.
A vertical skylight well that is above a kitchen island delivers good light directly over the work surface, but the narrow walls of the well limit the amount of light (left). By flaring the walls that tuck between the adjacent trusses, the same skylight delivers significantly more light to the room (right). The shaft walls are doing the lighting, not the skylight alone.

from flaring the shaft in all four directions. But even flaring the shaft in just one direction makes a difference. If you flare the side of the shaft that aligns with the upper edge of the skylight, it will give you the greatest increase in reflector area.

One of my favorite skylight applications is to place one low enough in a sloped wall that it becomes a window with a view (drawing below). For this placement to work, the sill of the skylight should be no more than 30 in. above the floor. By extending the sill horizontally into

Skylights can be windows, too.
By locating a skylight low in a sloped roof, it can do double duty as both skylight and window. The lower sill height effectively increases the size of the room and offers vistas that would otherwise be hidden from view. This can be accomplished with one large skylight or two stacked one above the other, as illustrated here.

the room at this height, you make a wide windowsill that is great for growing plants or sunning cats. Incidentally, with this kind of installation, it's also important to make the head of the opening parallel with the floor so that it maximizes the height of the opening and provides maximum reflector surface.

There are skylights on the market that are large enough to give you a reasonable head height for such a window. Alternatively, you can gang two skylights together vertically to make the head height equal to that of a typical window and still be able to operate the units.

If you keep in mind the idea that it's the sidewalls of the opening of the skylight that are really doing the work and not the skylight itself, you'll be able to get significantly more bang for your buck. And chances are you'll also get a lot of ooohs and aaahs from admiring friends and relatives, who'll be wondering why your skylight brings in so much more light than theirs, and looks better to boot.

What to Expect from Light Fixtures

Interior lighting is a key aspect of house design that frequently gets short shrift. Fixture selection is often ignored until the last minute when there's little time or money left to do it well. As a result, it's not unusual for a new home to have several fixtures missing or to have 79¢ porcelain bulb holders in conspicuous spots.

However, lighting is extremely important to the livability of a home, especially in northern climes, where for much of the winter, homeowners leave the house before dawn and return after sunset. Much of their experience of a house takes place when interior lighting is required.

Understanding available lighting options and knowing when selections need to be made can help designers, builders, and homeowners to develop a good lighting plan that integrates smoothly into the construction process. Although this article will introduce you to the basics, I'd also recommend that you pay a visit to your local lighting supplier to help fill out your knowledge base.

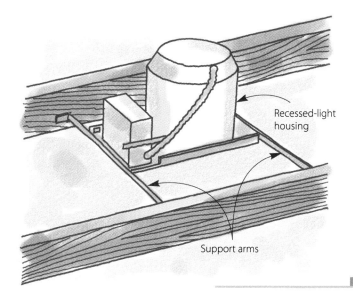

Recessed-light housing

Support arms

Recessed lights are adjustable. The recessed-light housing is set between joists by the electrician. The housing can be slid along the support arms, allowing fine adjustment before drywall installation.

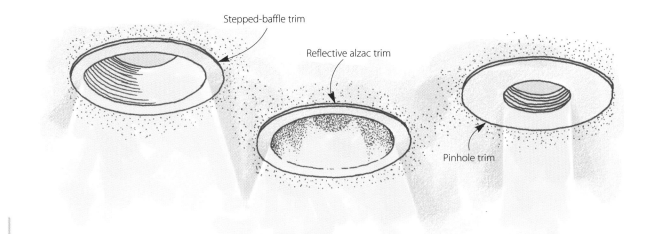

Stepped-baffle trim

Reflective alzac trim

Pinhole trim

Different trims for different tasks.
Trims are added into the housings toward the end of construction. The most common type is the stepped baffle. A more-expensive substitute is the highly reflective alzac trim. Pinhole trims direct light straight down in a tight beam to feature a special object.

Focusing on four broad light-fixture categories

I 'll focus on four fixture types: recessed, wall-mounted, ceiling-mounted, and track. I won't discuss hanging fixtures here because they are used mostly for decorative purposes.

The most prominently displayed fixtures in lighting showrooms are the wall- and ceiling-mounted varieties. But there are also plenty of recessed fixtures, or cans, that create distinctly different ambiences. These types of fixtures are rarely displayed well in showrooms because the fixtures themselves look unimpressive. The quality of light that they offer is notable but difficult to show in a warehouse full of light fixtures.

The same is true for certain types of wall-mounted fixtures (wall sconces). Although you'll see distinctly designed wall sconces in lighting showrooms, you'll rarely see incon-

spicuous fixtures that focus on getting light to where it's needed. Showroom fixtures are those that appeal to the largest number of people, but there are thousands of undisplayed fixtures available. A good lighting salesperson can find these fixtures for you, whether or not they are stock items.

The recessed can

A lso known as downlights, recessed cans are favorites in new homes. A series of recessed cans with flood lamps can light a room well. The focus is directed downward, lighting anything within the beam spread of the bulb. You should recognize, though, that recessed cans leave the ceiling unlighted.

Recessed lights are typically used to provide ambient light. For reading, you'll probably want a supplemental table or floor lamp that focuses light in just the right spot.

In a kitchen, however, recessed lights can provide excellent task lighting over islands or countertops.

The recessed can consists of two sections: the housing (drawing p. 115) and the trim. The electrician sets the housing before the installation of drywall, while the trim (drawing on the facing page) is the visible part that is placed at the end of construction. Typically, the interior surface of the trim, the baffle, is black or white, but it can also be silver, gold, or black alzac.

Because the housings are installed early in construction, it's important to design the lighting layout before construction begins. It is possible to add a can or two during construction, but cans are much easier to install before drywall is in place.

There are hundreds of different housings available, beginning with wide-diameter shallow fixtures, which are disliked by most designers because the bulb protrudes below the ceiling. At the other end of the spectrum are slot-aperture fixtures that all but disappear on the ceiling while brightly lighting the surface below.

Rather than enumerate all the possible options, I suggest that you ask lighting salespeople to show you several recessed-fixture catalogs. You can see options and decide what's best for your particular application.

Wall sconces can reflect light from the wall or the ceiling

Although wall sconces are typically decorative and provide a low level of light (drawing p. 118, left), other options exist. For example, halogen wall sconces provide general room lighting. The bulbs for these fixtures vary from 100 W to 300 W. Installed in a room with a broad, light-colored ceiling, the lights use the ceiling as a reflector (drawing p. 118, right). When installed with a dimmer, the lights in such rooms can be varied from daylight bright to candle charming. If you use this kind of wall sconce, it needs to be located higher on the wall than is typical of other types of wall fixtures so that the bulb itself is not visible. Make sure it is above the eye level of the tallest member of the household, say, 7 ft. from the floor.

The more common decorative wall sconces typically take 60 W or 100 W incandescent bulbs, whose light reflects from the wall. They're appropriate in bedrooms, hallways, and powder rooms or in any space whose ambience can be enhanced by a well-designed fixture. The mounting height varies from sconce to sconce, and I select these fixtures early so that the electrician can properly locate the rough wiring.

Standard sconce reflects from wall.

Off the wall.
Most residential wall sconces have a decorative design and provide ambience rather than whole-room lighting.

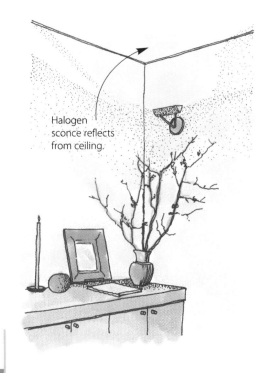

Halogen sconce reflects from ceiling.

Off the ceiling.
Many halogen wall sconces offer a low-key design and do an excellent job of lighting a room, especially when installed with a dimmer, using the ceiling as a huge reflector.

Surface-mounted ceiling fixtures are tough on ambience

Many older homes have surface-mounted ceiling fixtures throughout. Although they supply adequate lighting, they're generally a detriment to ambience. There's no subtlety to the light quality, and they can make occupants feel uncomfortable. The fixture is almost always visible, causing people to squint to see one another, and causing a general feeling that you're on display. For rooms that require good basic lighting but where the feel of the room is not critical, such as mudrooms, closets, and laundries, a ceiling fixture is an excellent choice. They're also a good strategy if dollars are tight.

Track lighting is a good remodeling option

The wiring for an existing ceiling fixture can often supply new track lighting (drawing facing page), which can better light a whole room. Track lights arranged to bounce light off a wall or ceiling, rather than pointing directly at a chair or couch,

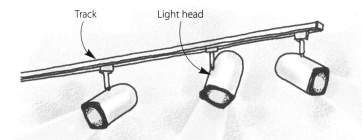

Track   Light head

Track lights are always adjustable.
Track lighting, once installed, gives homeowners the ability to remodel a lighting design whenever they wish. Fixtures can be added easily, and it's also a simple matter to change their orientation when desired.

provide more usable light. Also, you won't be spotlighting people, which can be an unpleasant experience. Track lighting is also an excellent choice to light a collection of paintings or family photos or to feature a wall hanging in a main living space.

As with recessed lighting, there are lots of fixtures to choose from. Because track lighting is generally easier to install than recessed, particularly in a remodel where the ceiling isn't being changed, it also can save money. Fixtures can be added to the track at any time, allowing the homeowner to alter the lighting design as money allows.

Good lighting design is worth the investment

Obviously, I've described only some available lighting options. There's much to know about bulbs, beam spreads and light quality. It's rare that residential-lighting design is done well, so rather than try to tackle it all yourself, I strongly recom-

mend that you find a knowledgeable guide. Many architects and interior designers are well versed in lighting design. For a project of significant scope and scale, a trained lighting designer is a wise investment. For most situations, however, your lighting showroom can give you the help you need.

Lighting is extremely important to the livability of a home, especially in northern climes, where for much of the winter, homeowners leave the house before dawn and return after sunset.

Locating Switches and Outlets

I call it "wall acne": all the switches, outlets, and electrical paraphernalia that scars the interior walls of a house. It's important to consider both long-term convenience and aesthetics when locating these things. The challenge is that electrical rough-in happens long before homeowners get a sense of the look and feel of a completed room. With no drywall in place in a house, it's a rare person who can visualize the cabinetry, furniture, and accessories that will fill the space after moving in.

A successful outcome requires good communication. Even when you perceive the job to be relatively small and straightforward, never assume that what you want is going to be obvious to the electrician. Walking through the house with the contractor and the electrician at the beginning of the electrical rough-in can help you avoid a lot of frustration and disappointment. Make sure that someone is taking good notes because there's typically a lot to remember.

Make switches handy but unobtrusive

Ask the electrician to locate all switches as close to the future door casing as possible (drawing facing page, top). This request may require that the contractor review with the electrician at the start of the job how far the final trim will extend. This step is especially critical if trim is unusually wide or if there is to be wall paneling.

The reason for this rule of thumb is twofold. First, when switches float in the wall far from the doorway, that wall is no longer usable as an unencumbered backdrop for art, furniture, or sculpture. Second, when you're entering or leaving a room, your hand tends to search for the switch near the door jamb. Groping for a switch in the dark is

I call it "wall acne": all the switches, outlets, and electrical paraphernalia that scars the interior walls of a house.

inconvenient and allows smudgy fingerprints to accumulate over time.

If several switches are needed in the same area, ask for them to be ganged together in a single box (drawings bottom right). If there are more than four switches, ask for two boxes, one above the other. Emphasize that you want the ganged boxes aligned vertically. When there are more than four switches in a row, it's difficult to remember which switch controls which fixture. The two tiers of switches give the brain more information. We tend to remember whether a switch was in the upper or lower bank and whether it was to the right of center or to the left.

Another function of the electrical walk-through is making sure that switches are located appropriately for the homeowners use patterns. This exercise can be over-whelming for many homeowners, so do your homework and have some recommendations in mind.

Tell the electrician where tall pieces of furniture, which might affect the locations of switches, might be placed. If there is a desk area or table planned, be sure to discuss the heights of outlets. Let the electrician know if you need an outlet above desk height in ad-dition to or in lieu of ones close to the floor.

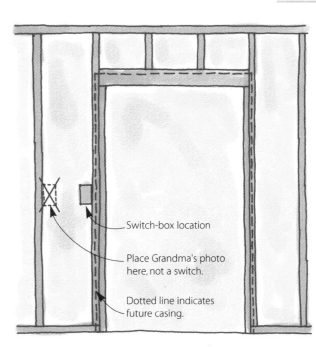

Switch-box location

Place Grandma's photo here, not a switch.

Dotted line indicates future casing.

Make switches handy and unobtrusive.
Locate switches as close to where the door casing will be installed as possible, which preserves wall space for artwork and makes finding the switch in the dark more intuitive.

Four switches in a row is the limit of most people's memory.

Gang multiple switches together.
More than four switches in one box, however, makes remembering which one does what difficult. Instead, stack more than four in two boxes. If there is an odd number of switches, add a dummy for symmetry.

Two rows of switches give our brains another clue to remembering the switches' functions.

Combined switch
and outlet

Switch plates are all
in the same line.

**Keep kitchen outlets
aligned horizontally.**
Keeping outlets at a consis-
tent height is particularly
important on tile walls.
Combining outlets and
switches in one box makes
the wall look less cluttered.

A good plan integrates outlets and finishes

Typically, unless otherwise specified, electricians locate outlets at around 12 in. above the floor and at the frequency required by code. Present-day codes call for outlets at least every 12 ft. and within 6 ft. of doors to avoid the need to string appliance cords across the room.

At kitchen counters, outlets are required every 2 ft., which means there will be a number of outlets along the backsplash (drawing left). These outlets can wreak havoc with any special tile design you may have planned. One solution is to work closely with the electrician to make sure that the outlets are carefully integrated with the tile design—not an easy task when you are still looking at rough framing. I prefer to run plug mold (a series of outlets set into a metal housing, as you sometimes see in a science lab) just below the upper cabinets (drawing facing page, left). This way, the outlets are out of sight but are convenient when needed.

Outlets are also required on kitchen islands. If you don't want an outlet to spoil the cabinetry design, be sure to review with the electrician where outlets should be located. Often, either end panel of the island is a good spot.

In bathrooms, a ground-fault protected outlet is required within 3 ft. of the sink. If

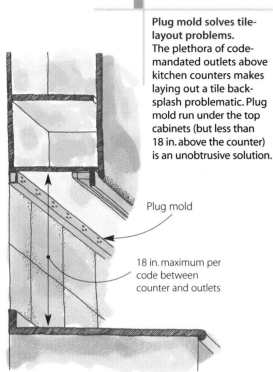

Plug mold solves tile-layout problems.
The plethora of code-mandated outlets above kitchen counters makes laying out a tile backsplash problematic. Plug mold run under the top cabinets (but less than 18 in. above the counter) is an unobtrusive solution.

Plug mold

18 in. maximum per code between counter and outlets

Not just any old spot works.
With their tight spaces and code-required outlets, bathrooms can be tricky places to locate outlets. Had this one been 6 in. farther from the mirror, it would have been covered by the hand towel.

Ground-fault outlet must be within 3 ft. of sink.

you have strong feelings about where these outlets should be located, tell your electrician. The location that seems right to you might not be obvious to anyone else. For example, some people prefer to set these outlets into the mirror. Others prefer the outlet on a side wall. If you are planning to hang a towel ring, the best place for the outlet is toward the back of the side wall (drawing above right).

In rooms with furniture arrangements planned far from adjacent wall surfaces, floor outlets are important to avoid a Rube Goldberg look. Envisioning the location of floor outlets can be tricky without furniture in place. It's an important-enough decision to

justify drawing the exact dimensions of the future furniture on the floor.

Locating outlets for special purposes such as floor lamps should be done at the rough-in phase. It's more expensive to add these circuits later, so planning early on can save a bundle. I recommend that homeowners and electricians or contractors make a list of unusual items that require outlets. Locate these items on the electrical plans, along with the desired height of each outlet off the floor.

Last, remember that, although these things may seem obvious to you, they aren't always clear to the electrician. A simple comment or two at the start of a job can save pricey alterations later.

SIX

Remodeling and Adding On

One of the most rewarding results of spreading the concepts behind building Not So Big has been hearing the stories people have to tell about how these ideas have saved them time and money. Many have realized they don't need more space, nor do they need to build new to create their dream home. They simply need to reallocate room functions so that all the spaces in the house can be used every day.

Although designing and building a new house can be a wonderful experience, it is definitely a major life event, requiring an immense amount of effort and energy, not to mention funds. For many people, remodeling or adding on is a much more manageable concept, especially if you basically like the place you're living in aside from a few shortcomings.

What follows will help you evaluate what to do with an existing house to make it really fit the way you and your family live. It will help you find the areas of the house that are currently underutilized and will give you the design tools needed to bring them to life. The trick is to start by identifying what works and what doesn't in the existing layout, and then to itemize the functions that you want to accommodate in the remodeled home. Only then should you start to think about physical solutions. And you'll get far more bang for the buck if you adopt the "less is more" approach, attempting to add only the minimum additional space to accomplish your goals.

This is a very different strategy from the standard process of adding on. Most people will start envisioning an addition to their home by drawing a big rectangle that extends the full width of the existing house and will then try to find the functions to fill that space. The result is invariably an addition that looks totally out of proportion to the rest of the house, that makes the existing rooms dark because it blocks the windows, and that is so big there's no coziness or intimacy to it. It might make a nice lobby for a commercial building, but it's lost all sense of home.

The strategies suggested here will turn the standard approach on its head, and allow you to put that important feeling of home at the top of the list rather than the bottom. By employing the simple ideas discussed here, you'll be able to achieve the home of your dreams without breaking the bank in the process.

Simple Floor-Plan Changes Can Revitalize an Older Home

In my book, *The Not So Big House: A Blueprint for the Way We Really Live,* I describe how the conventional house plan of today is ill-suited to our contemporary lifestyles. The formal spaces seldom get used in most households. Instead we gather in the kitchen and informal living spaces, even though these are typically the less well appointed areas of the house.

The book is a call for a new type of house, in which the "dinosaur" rooms are eliminated, and the dollars saved are used to make the spaces we use every day more comfortable, more personal, and more soulful. These concepts can be applied when building a new house, but they can also provide the guidelines for transforming existing space into the home you really want.

One of the most frequently asked questions that I hear is something like this: "If I have an older home without a family room, is there a way that I can make it work for present-day lifestyles?"

The answer in most cases is a resounding yes. Many homes built before the 1960s isolated the kitchen from the formal living areas—the living room and dining room—in order to keep odors and food prep away from the family's social space. This layout worked well in the days when wives were home all day and had time to prepare meals before husbands got home from work. With the advent of the two-income family, meal prep has become a more communal affair. Consequently, the kitchen has become the center of most homes, but it's frequently not laid out as such.

In older homes, the family still crowds into the utilitarian kitchen, and they wonder why the house feels so cramped! These kitchens were not designed for the purposes we put them to today. Many of them never housed family members at all. They were for the hired help, or the woman of the house, and they were certainly not considered places for sitting and socializing. Our lifestyles have completely metamorphosed, yet our houses still reflect the patterns of living from the turn of the last century.

So what do you do if you have such a home? How can you update it, to make the kitchen more hospitable, and to connect it with the dining and living spaces?

Separate rooms, waiting to break out of their isolation

Let's study two early twentieth-century floor plans to identify some governing concepts (drawings pp. 128 and 129). We see a standard central-stair colonial and a bungalow. Both have small kitchens, tucked off in the corner of each plan. They have clearly been designed to minimize interaction between kitchen and living room—exactly the opposite goal from our needs today.

Typically, if you can't see a space from the main congregating place, you are much less likely to use it. So the first order of business

Our lifestyles have completely metamorphosed, yet our houses still reflect the patterns of living from the turn of the last century.

is to open views from the kitchen to the other two living areas. The walls circled in red are places that could be opened up to make a visual connection.

Next we need to figure out what wall space is available for cabinetry. As was so frequently the case in kitchens of this era, there are doors entering the kitchen from several directions, making rearrangement of cabinetry and appliances quite a challenge. One important question to ask is if any doors can be moved or eliminated to open up a greater area of contiguous counter space.

Without adding any square footage, you can see that the kitchen in the colonial house has been significantly improved simply by moving the doorway between kitchen and dining room to the other side of the room (center drawing, p. 128). By doing this, a U-shaped kitchen results, which allows much better distribution of counter space.

In the example of the bungalow, with the inevitable and beautiful built-in buffet offering the only connecting wall between

Update a typical colonial floor plan by connecting the kitchen with other living spaces.
In the original plan (right), the walls circled in red close off the kitchen from other living spaces. Removing those walls, along with other changes shown below, establishes visual connections between the kitchen and adjacent rooms, opening them to the use that they deserve.

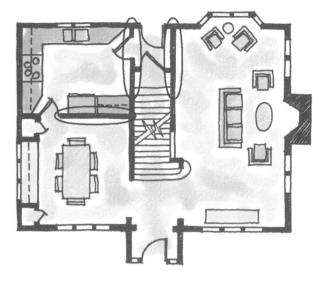

A pass-through to allow connecting views from the kitchen to the dining room

The walls of the stairwell have been opened up to allow connecting views from the kitchen to the living room.

Adding a bump-out to the plan improves the connection with the living area while simultaneously adding more counter space.

A peninsula counter with bar stools increases the relationship of the kitchen to the dining room.

kitchen and dining room, you might consider leaving the buffet. But take out the wall panel between lower and upper cabinets so that you can see through into the kitchen. If the buffet's upper cabinets are much lower than 4 ft. 8 in. at their base, you might replace them with smaller cabinets of the same design or eliminate them completely. If upper cabinets are too low to allow easy visual connection from one space to the next, they still function as a wall, and obstruct communication between spaces.

Frequently, the built-in buffet is one of the principal attractions in the purchase of such a house. To change it can seem like sacrilege. But remember that recrafting doesn't mean that it will be less than it was originally. With fine craftsmanship, the buffet can actually be made more, not less, beautiful.

In each of these examples, the formal dining room now serves both formal and informal purposes, and both living room and dining room can be seen from the kitchen, making them much more suited to the way we live today. Someone could be sitting in the living room in each case and conversing with a spouse in the kitchen. This interaction could not have happened in the unremodeled versions without a feeling of awkward separation.

A few years ago, I designed an addition to a colonial house with a plan similar to the one shown in the example. We remodeled the kitchen and added a family room beyond. In the process of the remodel, I suggested opening up the living room to the kitchen as shown here. The client was willing, but because she had never used this room in the past, she had a hard time believing that by simply removing the wall between the two, she would use the room any more frequently.

Once the addition was complete, I paid her a visit. To my amusement, the living room was now being used as the principal living space, and the new family room, we both realized, was an unnecessary luxury. She could simply have knocked out the wall between kitchen and living room to accommodate her needs and saved $50,000 in the process.

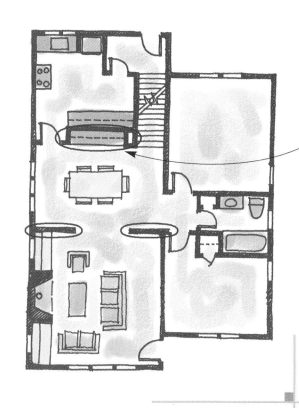

Open the wall above a built-in buffet rather than remove this signature detail.

A typical bungalow floor plan.
The areas circled in red are walls that can be altered to increase the connection between the kitchen, the living room and the dining room, as can be seen on the following page.

What happens if we add a little more square footage to these two kitchens?

Suppose the project's budget grows enough that we can afford to add a small amount of space to both of these houses. When people consider an addition, they frequently think big—adding a whole new room perhaps. But there are many less drastic and

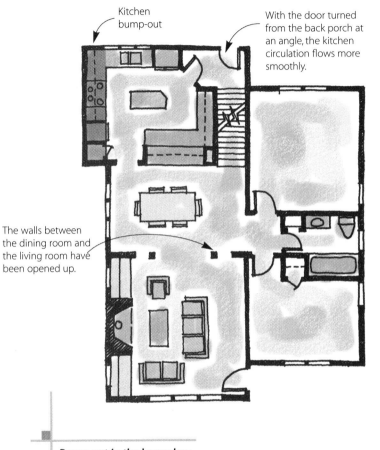

Kitchen bump-out

With the door turned from the back porch at an angle, the kitchen circulation flows more smoothly.

The walls between the dining room and the living room have been opened up.

Bump-out in the bungalow. By adding a bump-out that is a mere 30 in. wide by 15 ft. long to the side of the kitchen, the layout is dramatically improved.

less expensive options that can be used to improve a kitchen dramatically.

In both of these examples, a space has been added that is 2 ft. 6 in. wide and only 10 ft. to 15 ft. long. This sort of addition is often referred to as a bump-out. In each case, you can see that what results is a kitchen with space for a small island and, especially in the bungalow example, a significantly improved layout (drawing left). Because the existence of the built-in buffet made moving the door between kitchen and dining room undesirable, the addition of width to the kitchen lets cabinetry extend to this doorway without the need of an angled section of countertop, which always feels a little awkward.

The expanded kitchen in the colonial house is only slightly improved by the addition of space, but the connection between the kitchen and the living room is increased dramatically (bottom drawing, p. 128). This design would allow for easy conversation between both living room and dining room from the kitchen and would increase the overall sense of spaciousness far more than the additional 30 sq. ft. would imply. The bottom line: With a small amount of remodeling, you can make an older home meet today's lifestyle needs.

Making the Most of Your Remodeling Budget

It's a sad reality that almost everyone assumes their remodeling dollars will stretch farther than they realistically can. I can't tell you how many people have called me over the past few years saying, "We've finally decided to remodel with the $10,000 we've saved." That might sound like a lot of money, but when it comes to construction, that amount will allow only minor remodeling.

It seems that if you even breathe the word *remodel* at a kitchen these days, you're looking at a $50,000 project. How can this be? Aren't there ways to spend the money you've saved in a conservative way so that it accomplishes big enhancements without a hefty price tag?

Here are some remodeling rules of thumb, which I've gleaned from years of working with clients who have budgets that are somewhat (or even a lot) smaller than their dreams. Although you may not be able to attain a "perfect" solution to your home's problems when dollars are limited, you can make minor changes that will greatly enhance its livability.

Stay within the existing walls

In almost all cases, as soon as you add on, even a little, the price for the remodeling will jump dramatically. This cost increase is because exterior walls and windows are among the most expensive components of a house. When you puncture these walls, myriad issues have to be addressed, from structural integrity, to keeping the water out, to keeping the heat in. None of these things is cheap to do. Even if your house seems small and cramped, there are usually other ways to make it feel bigger that won't cost nearly as much as adding on.

Pinpoint the major problems

The problems that most people face in an existing house fall into these categories:

- Circulation problems
- Spatial problems
- Functional problems
- Aesthetic problems

I'll typically start by walking through the house with my clients and listening to what does and doesn't work for them. Often they'll think the only answer is adding on, but by taking a step back in the process, an architect or someone trained in design can identify a far less expensive solution.

For example, a common concern in many existing houses is a dysfunctional kitchen. In many older homes, the kitchen is chopped up with little or no usable counter surface and with appliances parked in awkward

places. Often there are so many doors opening into the room that there's no possibility of a continuous work surface. This problem is about circulation: too many pathways through the space, leaving not enough wall space for all the equipment and cabinetry that a kitchen requires.

Begin by asking yourself if there's a way that one or more of the doorways can be moved or removed to create more wall space. For example, if you can move a doorway between the kitchen and foyer so that it aligns with the back door at the other side of the kitchen, as shown in the plans on the facing page, you will be creating a U-shaped segment of wall that can greatly increase available counter space. This type of project will require relocating some electrical connections, but the plumbing—the most expensive utility work in kitchen remodeling—can stay put.

The cost of moving the doorway is relatively minor, but we rarely think of doing such a thing because we perceive a door as a fixed thing. The trick is to think beyond the boundaries of the problem room itself.

Another common problem is lack of coat-closet space on the main level, a particular concern in colder climates. By adding detail to an existing space, you sometimes can sneak in a closet at the same time. The drawings on p. 134 show how we borrowed a couple of feet from a dining room to add

Although you may not be able to attain a "perfect" solution to your home's problems when dollars are limited, you can make minor changes that will greatly enhance its livability.

Before remodel

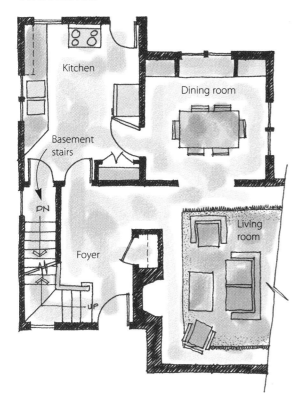

After remodel

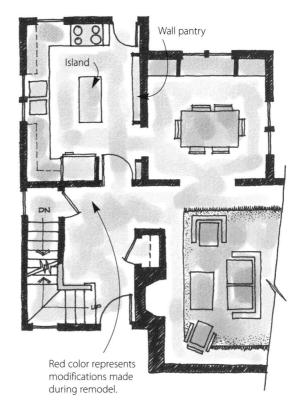

Red color represents modifications made during remodel.

two small closets connected by an archway. This example illustrates spatial as well as functional problems. The solution borrowed rarely-needed space to solve a more pressing need, and the archway added an elegant detail to the entry.

Identify underused areas

Because of certain cultural conventions, we tend to decorate rooms in fairly standard ways. The formal living room gets a couch, a couple of chairs and a coffee table. The formal dining room gets a dining table and six chairs, and a hutch if there's room. But often, these rooms aren't used

much, either because of the dictates of the furnishings or because the rooms can't be seen from the main living areas—usually the kitchen and the family room.

One of the most common additions today is a family room, a space that typically opens off the kitchen and that houses the TV, some comfortable seating, a coffee table, and sometimes a fireplace. A far less expensive approach to gaining this same space is to remodel the existing formal living room to accommodate these same needs. If there is only a wall between the kitchen and the living room, this remodeling is remarkably simple and inexpensive. By creating an opening

Moving two doors did the trick.
Moving the basement door into the foyer and relocating the foyer/kitchen door to align with the back door made a U-shaped counter possible. And moving the refrigerator made room for a kitchen island.

133

Before remodel

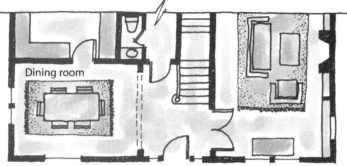

After remodel

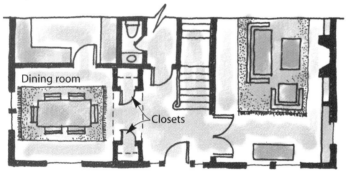

Smaller dining room, two closets.
By making the dining room—a rarely used space in this household—a little smaller, two closets were added. They are connected by a wide arch that enhances the sense of entry into the dining room.

such as an interior window between the two rooms, there's communication back and forth, as well as visual access (drawing facing page).

The dining room is another place that can serve other functions when not being used for formal dinners. Many people have far more books than bookshelves. How about lining the dining room with bookshelves, and allowing the room to double as a library, a place for mail-sorting and bill-paying, and a spot for doing homework? Just because the room is primarily designed for special occasions doesn't mean that's the only use you can put it to.

Often-overlooked strategies

This next piece of advice may seem so obvious that it's not worth mentioning, but I'm continually amazed that it's not implemented more often. If you find yourself short of space and your house is a mess, engage in some good old-fashioned housecleaning. Do it before you settle on a remodeling plan so that you'll at least know how much space you really need. Every residential architect will at some point wish he or she had the guts to say, "You don't need an addition. You need a cleaning service."

Finally, what if a room is too dark to be comfortable? This darkness might be due to a lack of windows, but that's not always the

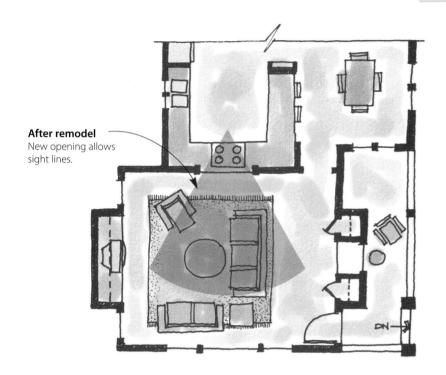

If you can see it, you're more likely to use it. By opening the wall between the kitchen and the formal living room, the need for a family-room addition (and a $50,000 investment) was eliminated.

After remodel
New opening allows sight lines.

case. If the room has a lot of dark wood-work, cabinetry or paneling, the problem might be solved with a coat of paint. Normally I love natural wood, but not when it creates a dingy, somber room. Painting a dark room can make a huge difference. It will suddenly become inviting and warm, and the house will seemingly increase in size as a result.

Whatever the problem, whether it's too much stuff, an awkward layout, or poor utilization of existing space, there's almost always a way to cure many of the greatest livability challenges even on a modest budget.

Every residential architect will at some point wish he or she had the guts to say, "You don't need an addition. You need a cleaning service."

Getting the Most from a Ranch without Adding On

If you live in a ranch-style house (sometimes called a rambler), chances are good that you've wondered how to make it feel more comfortable and more tailored to today's lifestyles. The ranch took hold across the country shortly after World War II, providing young families with reasonably priced housing and a slice of the American Dream. But although these houses offered shelter and convenience, they did not have a lot of frills—and

they still don't. To keep prices affordable, exterior forms were simple, most frequently a long thin rectangle with a shallow-pitch roof (drawing below). Interior decor was limited to simple casings around windows and doors, and not much else.

Neighborhoods of such homes have, for the most part, aged gracefully. Residents often want to stay in their neighborhood and community but long for a nicer home. And ranch houses have proved difficult to

Ranch houses were affordable but plain.
A typical post–World War II ranch, or rambler, was a no-frills way for many Americans to buy a house for the first time. Relatively simple changes can enliven interior spaces and make the house more comfortable.

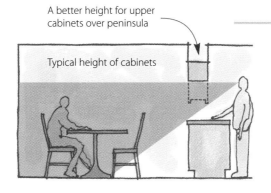

A better height for upper cabinets over peninsula

Typical height of cabinets

Low cabinets block eye contact.
Kitchen designs often include low-hanging cabinets over a peninsula that obscures an adjacent eating area. Raising the upper cabinets clears sight lines to other parts of the house and makes the space work better.

update. Assuming they need an addition, homeowners look to builders and architects to help them, but there's definitely a dearth of remodeling possibilities short of a major (read: expensive) overhaul.

The motivation may not be a need for more space as much as it is a desire to reconfigure the house and make it more attractive. I strongly believe that you should first look at what can be done with existing space to increase its livability before deciding to build an addition.

The following concepts can all be implemented without extending the ranch house beyond its current form.

Open the kitchen to adjacent spaces, and replace small windows

Most ranch homes were designed when the kitchen was used primarily by the woman of the house while the rest of the family was at work or school. Usually, the kitchen is separated from the living room and dining room, and there is no other informal living space. Although there is often a small kitchen eating area, it is frequently separated from the kitchen by low cabinetry above a peninsula. Families may spend much of their time here, but they strain to see each other as they move between kitchen work area and table.

So the very simplest first step to making the kitchen work better for today's lifestyles is to raise the height of those cabinets over the peninsula. Removing obstructions to clear sight lines between main living areas is key to making the space you have work better (drawing above).

Cabinetry in the ranch kitchen is often bare bones and unappealing. There are many things that can be done to update it, from adding a coat of paint to completely replacing the old stuff with new. Simply getting rid of darker finishes and old appliances in once-trendy colors (gold and avocado) makes an amazing difference.

People often update [ranches] by adding on. But the motivation may not be a need for more space as much as it is a desire to reconfigure the house and to make it more attractive.

New soffits help to define the room.
Two-ft. wide soffits around the perimeter of this kitchen give the room a clearer definition without using walls. The soffit also provides a place for task lighting.

Instead of moving cabinets and appliances to make a better work area, less-expensive approaches may have more impact. Adding a 2-ft.-wide soffit above the cabinets, for example, gives the room more spatial definition (drawing above) and provides an excellent place for task-oriented recessed lighting. I avoid soffits that stop abruptly, as though they've been sliced through. If you can make the soffit continuous around the room, the space will look and feel better.

Another fairly simple kitchen modification is to make the windows larger. Ranch-house windows often are small and too high

off the floor to see out of comfortably. (This problem is also often true of bedroom windows in these homes.) By increasing the size and lowering the sill height, the kitchen and eating area can be vastly improved. If the sill can be set at roughly table height (30 in.), you'll get a far greater connection with the outdoors. Finally, if you can open a view from the kitchen to the dining room or living room (or both), you will find that you start to use much more of the house for everyday living. The rule is that if you can see a space, you are much more likely to use it.

Get rid of the boxiness by varying ceiling heights

Many ranch-house residents are frustrated by the feeling that they are living in a series of boxes, all the same height. Owners often want to increase the ceiling height of some rooms. But because these houses often were built with roof trusses, this plan is difficult to accomplish structurally, and it can be costly. The alternative, which can be equally or more effective, is to lower ceilings in places to create some variety.

Adding soffits around the perimeter of a room defines the space (just as it did in the kitchen) and makes the center of the room feel taller because we experience it in contrast to the lowered ceiling. I will typically

Lowering part of the ceiling makes a more interesting space.
One fix for the boxy interior of a typical ranch house is to lower one end of a long thin room to create two activity places rather than one. This kind of change simultaneously improves the proportions of the room.

locate the soffit directly above door and window heads, or directly above the surrounding casing. If a room is long and thin, you can lower one end, say, 8 ft. out from the wall to define two activity places within the room (drawing above).

Ranch houses often have long hallways with 8-ft. ceilings. They usually have minimal lighting and feel uninviting. By lowering the ceiling to around 7 ft., adding some recessed lighting at 6-ft. (or so) intervals along the way, and spotlighting a painting or wall hanging at the end of the hall, the space is transformed. It no longer feels like a dark tunnel, and the light at its far end draws you in and makes you feel welcomed.

Get rid of ranch-style casings

Perhaps the most unloved characteristic of the ranch house is the "ranch-style" casing that surrounds all windows and doors. It was designed to be simple and inexpensive. One of the most effective ways to change the character of a ranch house is to replace this trim. If you are a fan of prairie-style architecture, for example, you can run a continuous band of flat casing above doors and windows, using standard widths of 2¼ in. or 3½ in. in thicknesses from ⅜ in. to ¾ in. You can use any wood that's readily available, or you can use MDF (medium-density fiber board) and paint it. The result is a much more tailored look (drawing p. 140, top).

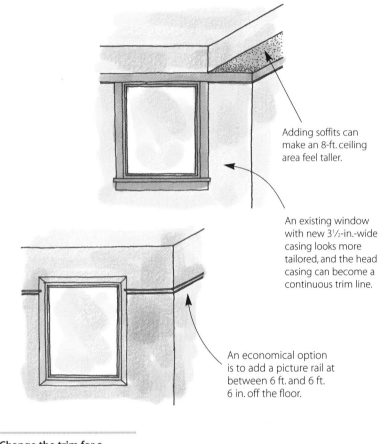

Adding soffits can make an 8-ft. ceiling area feel taller.

An existing window with new 3½-in.-wide casing looks more tailored, and the head casing can become a continuous trim line.

An economical option is to add a picture rail at between 6 ft. and 6 ft. 6 in. off the floor.

Change the trim for a better look.
Keeping the trim simple helps to keep costs down. An easy way to improve the look of a ranch-house interior is upgrading door and window casing. When you're adding a picture rail, paint the wall area above the rail the same color as the ceiling; then paint the area below the trim line another color.

Because not all doors and windows are set at the same height, you can run this band at the highest head height. Then, where there are lower head heights, add a filler trim piece. This plan ties everything together beautifully.

If you don't want to replace all the existing trim, you can add what is referred to as a backband to surround the casing and base. This alternative will draw more attention to the woodwork, and it will make larger frames for all door and window openings.

If you like the idea of the continuous trim line to tie things together, you can then add a narrow piece of picture mold somewhere between 6 ft. and 6 ft. 6 in. off the floor to give a similar effect at much lower cost (drawing bottom). When using this detail, I like to paint the area above the line the same color as the ceiling and the area below the line a somewhat contrasting color.

None of the above strategies costs a lot of money, yet each can have a huge impact on the personality and livability of the ranch. So before you go about the process of adding on, give these concepts some careful consideration; they could save you a bundle and actually make your house work better for you (with much less disruption) than a full-blown addition.

Expanding a Ranch: Adding Up or Adding Out?

Owners of ranch-style homes often see adding on as an opportunity to dramatically change the home's appearance with a second story. But starting the planning process with a preconceived notion of the outcome is a common mistake. It is far better to start by identifying what spaces you would like, but don't currently have, to help you avoid adding more room than you really need. You may discover that a smaller addition suits your needs much better than a new second floor, and costs less.

You may discover that a smaller addition suits your needs much better than a new second floor, and costs less.

First, know thy setback rules

When adding on, lot constraints can be a big consideration. Knowing your property lines as well as local setback requirements will define the boundaries of what you will be allowed to add to your house. Each town and city has its own set of regulations specifying how close a building (or addition) may be to property lines. The rules help maintain a certain look and feel to a neighborhood, and they prevent houses from being built too close to one another.

If an addition you are contemplating will encroach into a setback area, you will need to apply for a variance. Even minor encroachments may not be granted, so don't assume that a variance will automatically be given. Many cities are cautious about setting precedents they will later regret, so they tend to be more conservative in their approvals than most homeowners anticipate.

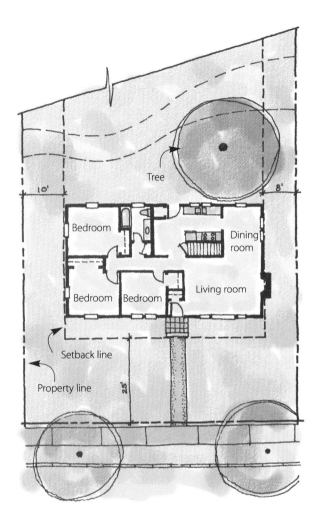

Start with an accurate site plan.
A plan showing property and setback lines, major vegetation, and topography is the starting point for deciding where and how to add square footage to this ranch-style house. Note that the existing chimney encroaches into the setback area.

To identify where property lines, setback lines, and house are, you need a property survey. In fact, it may be required. Obtaining one early in the design process makes the work of an architect, designer, or builder easier, so it's best to obtain one before design work starts.

If you live in an area with small lots, you should also ask the surveyor to locate the edges of adjacent buildings so that you can design with them in mind. You might ask the surveyor to indicate where major vegetation

is located, as well as any significant topography. The resulting plan (drawing left) allows you to tailor any new addition to the shape of the land.

Deciding whether to build a new second floor or to add out

Now, with your list of desired spaces and an understanding of the constraints of the lot, you are ready to take a look at where to locate your addition. Sometimes this solution is straightforward. For example, you want to add a family room that needs to be close to the existing kitchen. There are no constraints in the backyard, so you know almost immediately where the addition needs to go.

But things often are more complicated. To illustrate the process of deciding whether to add up or out, let's take a house and a desire for an addition, and place it on two different lots with different site constraints. Here's the building problem we're trying to solve:

The existing house is a 1950s ranch with a floor plan that separates the kitchen from the dining room and the living room (drawing above). As a result, these two rooms are seldom used. The owners want a family room for watching TV and for family socializing, and they also want a master-bedroom suite, ideally on the main level, with plenty

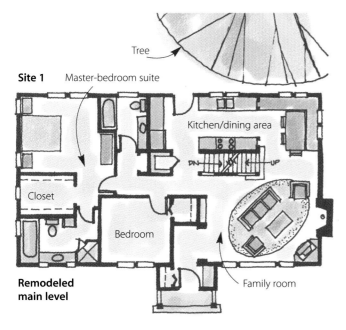

Tree

Site 1

Master-bedroom suite

Kitchen/dining area

Closet

Bedroom

**Remodeled
main level**

Family room

Altering the main level for a flat site.
Because of a favorite tree in the backyard, this site encouraged the alteration of the existing first-floor plan and the addition of a new second level that would include new bedroom space as well as a home office and a new library.

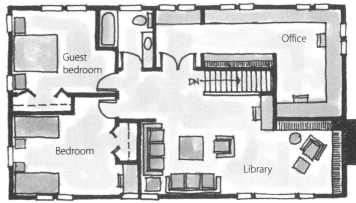

A new upper level

Guest
bedroom

Office

Bedroom

Library

of closet space and a separate bath with both shower and soaking tub. Currently, all three bedrooms share the same bathroom. The husband is doing an increasing amount of work from home, and he would like an in-home office if possible. The wife would like to do some graphic-design work in the same space, so the office area needs to be generously sized. Because the couple's two children occupy the other two bedrooms, they would also like to add a guest bedroom with a bathroom close by. This bedroom could be on any level.

We have two imaginary sites to work with. At site 1, the lot is flat, but in the backyard, there is a large oak tree that the owners do not want to lose. The rear property line is close to the house. At site 2, the lot abuts a scenic river valley, and the backyard falls away from the house rapidly. Views from this side of the house are excellent.

On site 1, after reviewing options with their architect, the family decides to remodel the existing living room into the desired family room (drawing above left), to create a master-bedroom suite and to add up. A new second floor includes an upstairs library/sitting room, a new guest bedroom, a bedroom that was displaced by the first-floor alterations, and an in-home office (drawing above right). The tree is untouched by construction.

On site 2, the family elects to add out (drawing p. 144). The addition includes a new family room, and master closet and bathroom, both of which open into the adjoining master bedroom. Because of the significant slope of the site, a lower level is

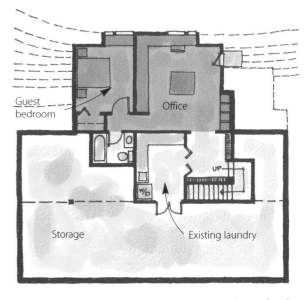

Site 2

Guest bedroom

Office

Storage

Existing laundry

Main level

Lower level

For a sloped site, add out. On the main level, an addition includes space for a new family room, closet, and bathroom. Because the lower level would have to be built anyway, space here is inexpensive. The lot allows for a walk-out home office, along with a guest bedroom.

necessary, and this area becomes the in-home office, accessed by a new stair that is part of the addition (drawing above right). The new guest bedroom is also on this level.

What typically happens when no one considers how much space is really needed or how existing spaces can be modified? In the example using site 2, you might find the owners adding the family room plus a second floor, which would be significantly more expensive and would not serve the owners' needs as well. The space below the family room, which is cheap space because it has to be there anyway, would remain unused, despite its excellent views to the river. And the upstairs would remain fairly cavernous, waiting for a function and, in all probability, the money to finish it and decorate it properly.

Unless you are planning to add as much square footage as the main level of your existing house, it is probably going to be less expensive and less disruptive to your lives to add out rather than add up. However, if you have certain site constraints or if you need a significant amount of new space, up may be the way to go.

Start with a rigorous analysis of what you really need, and more often than not, you'll find yourself adding out, with a smaller addition than you thought you needed. It probably will work better than a bigger but less carefully considered addition.

The Art of Adding On

For optimal results, you need to question your initial assumptions, even if these seem unassailable to you. It's these assumptions that most frequently get us into trouble and make us think we need much more space than we really do.

We've all seen them, those misbegotten appendages to originally charming older homes. Perhaps it's an addition with absolutely no aesthetic resemblance to the original house, or perhaps it's a new segment of space that is ill-proportioned and dwarfs the rest of the structure. You drive past and think, "How could they do that to such a lovely old house?"

Chances are the owners didn't mean to. They just didn't know how to ask for something that fit the existing home better. The typical process goes as follows:

Mr. and Mrs. Jones have a charming house that's a little too small (drawings p. 146). They figure that they need an 18-ft. square space for their new family room. So they call in a local builder who says that yes, he can do that, but because the house is actually 36 ft. wide, why not make that new addition

For optimal results, you need to question your initial assumptions, even if these seem unassailable to you. It's these assumptions that most frequently get us into trouble and make us think we need much more space than we really do.

Rear elevation of the original house.
Modest in size and detail, this prim little house nevertheless has a dignified and coherent exterior.

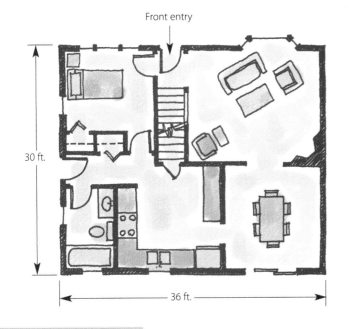

Front entry

30 ft.

36 ft.

Original floor plan.
Cramped and compartmentalized, the original floor plan lacks space for hanging out near the kitchen.

go all the way across the back (drawings facing page)? "Okay," say the homeowners. "We could certainly use the space."

A drawing is done by the builder or an in-house draftsperson. A building permit is acquired. Prices are obtained. Construction starts. What was left out? Absent from this process is any discussion about actual space needs, about how the new space will affect use of existing spaces, about how to integrate the addition with the existing house, or about aesthetic characteristics of both interior and exterior. In other words, design has been omitted from the equation.

Find a designer who will ask a lot of questions

We assume that houses aren't that complicated. Because most of us have lived in them all our lives, we believe we know what we need. But familiarity is not the same as expertise. Some builders have an innate design capability, but most freely acknowledge that their skill is in the act of building and crafting, and that they are happiest when they build someone else's design.

So the first step in adding on to a home should be to find a designer. This person needs to be a good listener. Often, what you think you need and what you actually need are two very different things.

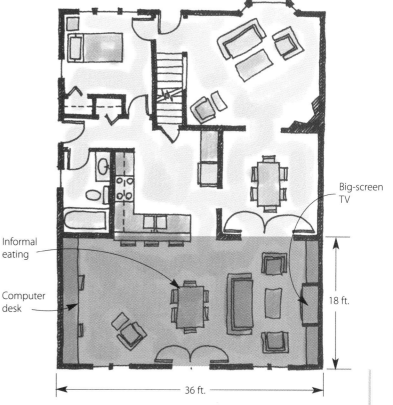

Dueling rooflines.
Can we agree that this is ugly?
Extending the full width of the
house, this bulky addition bears
no stylistic resemblance to the
original house, creating an
uneasy alliance between the two.

Big-screen
TV

Informal
eating

Computer
desk

18 ft.

36 ft.

The homeowners, for example, wanted to
add a family room. But their analysis of their
own needs was perfunctory. It could be sum-
marized as "we need more space." An architect or home designer will probe further, asking questions such as these:

- How much money do you have to spend
  on the project?

- Where do you spend your time in the
  house currently?

- What are the activities that are not accommodated adequately by the space you
  have now?

- Is it important that the new family-
  gathering space be open to the kitchen,
  or would you prefer that the kitchen be
  separate from it?

- Is a rear entry to be part of the addition?

- Are there any concerns about connection
  to a garage or carport?

- Do you want to be able to get to the backyard from this new addition to the house?

- Are there other rooms in the house that
  should be visible from this new room?

- Do you currently have a main-level guest
  powder room?

- If not, do you want to add one now, while
  there is construction going on in the
  house?

- Should the new space look and feel like
  the older parts of the house, or do you
  want to establish a new character and
  look for the new space?

**More addition than
necessary.**
By spanning the entire width
of the house, this addition
provides lots of space. But it
doesn't take into consideration the function of the old
living room and dining
room. What's more, it doesn't
fit with the character of the
house.

An addition that enhances the house.
Instead of competing with the original house, this solution complements it. The smaller roof reinforces the shape of the old one, and the horizontal trim lines help to integrate the new and old work.

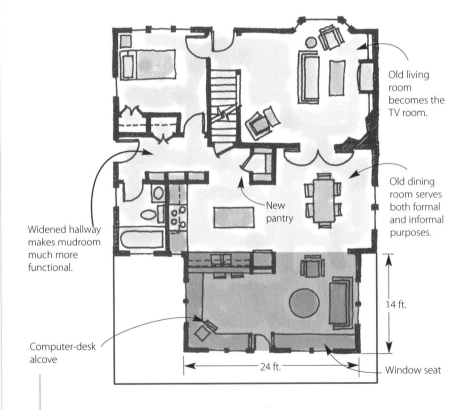

Old living room becomes the TV room.

Old dining room serves both formal and informal purposes.

New pantry

Widened hallway makes mudroom much more functional.

Computer-desk alcove

14 ft.

24 ft.

Window seat

A scaled-back solution.
Although it is significantly smaller than the first proposal, this addition works better by integrating the original rooms into the new floor plan.

- Are there spaces that are currently used for activities that will move to the new addition?

- What do you plan to do with these vacated spaces once the new area is built?

- Is there a way to open these spaces to the new addition so that you don't need to add as much new space?

- Will there be any need to redecorate these existing spaces to integrate them with the character of the new space?

- Is there a need for mudroom space?

And then there are the questions that architects or designers will ask themselves, questions that most homeowners will not have thought of:

- What are the property-setback requirements?

- Is there special vegetation that will be affected by the addition?

- What is the orientation of the existing house, and what does that suggest for the window locations and the sun penetration in the new addition?

- Where are neighbors' houses located, and how will they affect views from windows in the new addition?

- How will the new addition affect neighbors' views?

- What is the roof of the existing house like, and what roof forms will look best when added to it?

This last question is one of the most critical in terms of aesthetics. And yet it is the one that is most frequently omitted. An addition designed without consideration of this important issue typically looks like a mistake. So a good rule of thumb is to ask this question first, and then design the inside layout to correspond to the exterior solution (drawings facing page).

Although most designers and architects will work on both the interior and the exterior simultaneously, for the nondesigner, this concept helps put the appropriate emphasis on the issue of roof form and shape of addition. The ultimate compliment for an addition is to have friends ask, "Now where did you add on?" The new space and form integrate so well with the existing structure that it's not clear where old stops and new starts. And frequently, the added space is smaller (and less expensive) than what the homeowners envisioned, though it serves them better.

Sometimes, the space is already there

A few years ago, I visited a couple who were planning a family-room addition. When I arrived at the front door, and was received into the living room, I was quite taken aback. The living room was completely empty of furniture, and the drapes were closed. The homeowner took me back into the kitchen, which was filled to the gills with stuff. Then she started to tell me about her dreams of a family room.

I hesitantly asked her why she didn't use her living room. "Oh," she said, "it's so dark." I inquired if she had thought about opening the drapes. She looked surprised, as though I'd suggested something she'd never even thought of. "But we are so close to the neighbors' house," she said. "We look right into the side of their house, and there's no privacy."

I suggested that she invest in some art glass for the living-room windows, which would let in the daylight but keep out the view. In addition, I suggested opening up the wall between the kitchen and the living room. That solution would give the living room the same function as a family room and would cost only a fraction of the proposed addition—I'd just saved them at least $50,000 with a one-hour consultation.

Not all consultations end up having that kind of return on investment, but the message is an important one. For optimal results, you need to question your initial assumptions, even if these seem unassailable to you. It's these assumptions that most frequently get us into trouble and make us think we need much more than we really do. Looking at the house as an integrated whole and making sure that every space in the house is used effectively can help reduce the amount of additional space required.

When Adding On, Let the Roof Be Your Guide

Whether you have a Craftsman bunga-low, a Cape Cod saltbox, or an American foursquare, when it comes to adding on, it's important to make the new addition fit with the existing house. Although this fact sounds obvious, it's amazing how rarely it happens.

One of the additions that bothered me most in my old neighborhood was a house where the shed dormers had been extended to the home's gable end. The siding was then redone, and all indication of the juncture between the original dormers and the rest of the house was concealed. What resulted was a house that looked monumental, ill-propor-tioned, and just plain ugly (drawings facing page). Seeing houses added onto in this way is so sad. All the charm of the original house is lost in the name of adding a few square feet, and "modernizing."

When most people add on, they develop the floor plan first and then wonder how to roof it. This is backward thinking. With additions, you have to start with the roof and then work to see what can be done with the floor plan. Here are some real-life examples.

The typical approach to additions—adding the most space for the lowest price—is a guarantee that the new space will shriek "addition" to you and to your neighbors.

Ignoring the original rooflines can lead to bad results.
Before.
This house, with its random assortment of rooflines, still had its own idiosyncratic charm until…

After.
…The owners extended the dormers to the gable end, creating an ungainly facade. This addition was designed from the inside, with no thought to the exterior appearance.

Expanding a Prairie-style house

A couple with three children came to our office a few years ago wanting to remodel their kitchen and to add a family room with a new master-bedroom suite above. The existing house was an American foursquare with prairie-style overtones (drawings p. 152).

We looked at several roof options for the new addition, but in this case, the only one that really looked good was a two-story addition with a hip roof to match the roof of the existing house. Issues such as window placement, style, and pattern were also important to make the addition fit with the existing structure.

Adding a gable-roof form to this house obviously wouldn't look good. By matching the overhang width and gutter details from the old house, the new space blends seamlessly into the home. Once the roof was selected, we worked with the floor plan to determine how far to extend from the existing house, but the width was predetermined because we didn't want to cover the windows in the sunroom.

Look to windows, trim detail, and roof shapes for guidance. Before.
This house has a hip roof and some exterior trim lines, giving it a prairie-style character. The flat-roofed bump-out houses a sunroom that the owners didn't want to lose.

After.
The addition has a hip roof as well as many of the details that give this home its character. Note that the addition abuts the sunroom, allowing it to remain unaltered.

Adding some style to a plain little house

A couple with a simple story-and-a-half stucco home came to us looking for a way to increase the size of the existing kitchen and to add an eating area, a mudroom, and a small office space. They had assumed that this project would be a one-story addition, but they were worried about losing too much of their backyard because they were avid gardeners. Looking at their budget, I knew that we would have to keep the addition compact. In checking out their expectations on the size of office space

required, we discovered that they needed little more than an alcove, though bookshelves were important. By adding a gabled addition of just 6 ft. by 12 ft., all their needs were met. The key was to place the entrance to the office space off the stair landing, three steps down from the second floor, allowing the addition to stay small by minimizing circulation space. The very plain back of the house gained a far more attractive facade in the process (drawings facing page).

Sometimes a small addition can have a big impact on style.
Before.
About the only details that needed to be retained on the back of this house were the two windows on the left, which flanked the buffet in the dining room.

After.
In plan, this addition measures a mere 6 ft. by 12 ft., but it has transformed the house and pre-served precious backyard gardening space. The two dining-room windows have been retained, and the gable shape and trim details repeated.

Preserving warmth while expanding a small house

A family with a house that looked like an English country cottage was planning to move because they didn't have enough space and couldn't imagine how to add on without wrecking the look of the house. Although our solution was not cheap, we showed them a way to add on that would enhance rather than detract from the existing roof forms. Considering the costs of moving and finding a larger, equally comfortable house, they realized that the addition was the more economical approach. The key to this solution was to add on to both the dormer form and the house form. A two-story gabled addition houses a family room with a master bedroom above. The continuation of the shed dormer is the key to this solution (drawing p. 154). Without it, the addition looked tacked on.

In each of the above solutions, we used the following thought process. Ask yourself the same questions.

1. The roof of the house suggests the roof shapes of the addition. What are the existing roof forms like? Gable? Hip? Shed?

2. Are there existing windows that would be a loss to the interior experience of the house if they were covered up by the new

Modest dormers retain the scale of a one-and-a-half-story house.
Because they stop well shy of the gable end, the shed dormers atop this gable roof don't appear top heavy. The row of French doors in the addition helps to preserve the cottage feeling of the house.

addition? This establishes the limits of the addition's width.

3. What are the existing overhangs, window patterns, and other exterior details like? The answers establish general characteristics of the addition, unless the existing face of the house could use some help.

4. Are there any opportunities offered by the interior configuration of the existing house that allow for a more creative solution than initially envisioned? For instance, coming off the stair landing to make a small office space above the new eating area, rather than adding a larger single-story addition.

If, as you plan your own addition to your home, you follow these simple guidelines, seeking always to add the least space to accomplish the most internal improvement, you'll find that your addition fits the house to a tee, and you'll have more money available to give it some real personality. The typical approach to additions—adding the most space for the lowest price—is a guarantee that the new space will shriek "addition" to you and to your neighbors.

Start with the existing roof, let it guide you in the design of the addition, keep the details and scale in line with what's already there, and take the opportunity to add a little personality and proportion. It's also the best way to secure the investment in your home. Good-looking additions sell far better than ugly ones.

Afterword

So now you know almost as much about making your home function better as any architect or builder. Don't be deceived though. Just because you understand where the problems are and what solutions might be appropriate, it doesn't mean you won't benefit from professional help with design and implementation. The professionals you select can have an enormous impact on the relative success of the project.

There are many architects, interior designers, builders, and craftspeople across the country—and even around the world—who have come out of the woodwork to express their support for the values espoused in *The Not So Big House* and *Creating the Not So Big House*. The challenge up until recently has been finding the appropriate people in your particular area. You can check with your local chapters of the AIA (American Institute of Architects), ASID (American Society of Interior Designers), NAHB (National Association of Homebuilders), and NARI (National Association of the Remodeling Industry). But many of the best are small businesses that are not members of their local or national professional organizations, making them difficult to find unless you know someone personally or get a word-of-mouth recommendation.

So in an attempt to facilitate this search, the Not So Big House web site (www.notso-big.com) includes a database of professionals and artisans who would like to be considered for such work. There are many links on the site, as well as additional information to help you make your home all that it can be. There's also an active Community Bulletin Board that will allow you to compare notes with others who are engaged in the same kinds of home projects as you.

The concepts discussed in the preceding pages can be implemented regardless of your budget. Good solutions to everyday house headaches don't have to cost an arm and a leg to be successful. The ones you usually see in the house and home magazines tend to be at the upper end of the economic spectrum, but the ideas they embody can still be applied to much simpler projects.

Some of the most wonderful dwelling places I've visited will never appear in print, but they've got that certain something that lets you know they're deeply loved and cared for. Make your home an expression of yourself, and you'll find it feeds your spirit in ways you'd never imagined possible.